RIDE ON!

DAME SARAH STOREY'S EXTRAORDINARY JOURNEY OF TRIUMPH: HOW TO UNLEASH THE POWER WITHIN, PUSH BOUNDARIES, AND CHAMPION EXCELLENCE

S. A. STERLING

Disclaimer Notice

This book, "Ride On! Dame Sarah Storey's Extraordinary Journey of Triumph," is an independent publication written by S.A. Sterling and is intended solely for educational and entertainment purposes. The material contained within aims to provide readers with a comprehensive understanding of Dame Sarah Storey's life experiences and achievements, as well as impart various life lessons for personal growth and betterment.

While all reasonable efforts have been made to ensure the accuracy and reliability of the information presented, neither the author nor the publisher can guarantee its completeness, timeliness, or applicability to all individuals or situations. The author and publisher specifically disclaim any liability, loss, or risk, personal or otherwise, that may be incurred as a direct or indirect consequence of the application and execution of any content, advice, or recommendation included herein.

This book is not a substitute for professional guidance or counseling and should not be interpreted as such. The viewpoints, interpretations, and conclusions expressed are those of the author and do not necessarily represent the views, policy, or facts as acknowledged by any entity, organization, or person cited or referenced. All readers are encouraged to seek qualified professional advice before making any decisions based on the information contained in this book.

By reading this book, you acknowledge that the author and publisher are not responsible for your actions and decisions, and you agree to release them from any form of liability with respect to errors, omissions, or inaccuracies in the content.

TABLE OF CONTENTS

SNEAK PEEK:
UNCOVER THE TRIUMPH

Journey through the extraordinary life of Dame Sarah Storey and discover the power of triumph over adversity.

The Finish Line

The Cyclist's Spirit

Defying limits

 Her attitude is what really made her a great champion. She had this unmatched self-determination and ability to self-reflect on her achievements.

Continue the journey at
www.sasterling.com

What you will gain from Ride On

- **Unlock the Power of Resilience** - Unearth the key traits and habits that have propelled Dame Sarah Storey through the hurdles of life and into the annals of sports history.

- **Discover Untapped Potential** - Journey through Sarah's life to unearth valuable lessons on how you too can go beyond your perceived limitations.

- **Empower Yourself** - Our narrative dissects Dame Sarah Storey's experiences to deliver essential empowerment techniques, which you can incorporate into your own life.

- **Achieve personal growth** - Internalize real-world wisdom on triumph over adversity, personal transformation, and what it means to achieve true greatness.

- **Inspire to Aspire** - Whether you're an athlete, a dreamer, or someone who loves an excellent underdog story, 'Ride On!' is a catalyst for action and inspiration.

Why this book is for you

- **RAW & REAL** - Unearth the key traits and habits that have propelled Dame Sarah Storey through the hurdles of life and into the annals of sports history.

- **ACTIONABLE TAKEAWAYS** - Beyond just storytelling, this book provides actionable tips, wisdom, and insights that you can apply directly to your own journey towards success.

- **DIVERSE APPEAL** - Whether you're into sports, personal development, or simply love a gripping life story, 'Ride On!' has something special for you.

So, are you ready? If you're looking to be inspired, educated, and transformed, then don't miss out on this extraordinary story of an extraordinary woman.

RIDE ON, RIDER, RIDE ON!

Unlock your exclusive
GIFT & RESOURCES!

Hey there, Amazing Reader!

Thank you for picking up "Ride On! Dame Sarah Storey's Extraordinary Journey of Triumph." To express our gratitude, we've got an exclusive gift and resources specially curated for you!

What's in Store for You?

● **BONUS: Free eBook Guide "EmpowerHER: Journey to Self-Discovery"**
Your ultimate roadmap to women's empowerment, resilience, and personal transformation.

● **Personal Growth Worksheets**
Your practical, step-by-step guide to achieving greatness, tailored just for you.

● **New! BLOG: Women Rising Strong**
Dive into awe-inspiring stories of remarkable women, meticulously curated to elevate your spirit.

How to Access?
It's simple! Click the link below to be redirected to www.sasterling.com and enter your email address to unlock your exclusive gifts and resources.

Visit www.sasterling.com to unlock your gift

FOREWORD

Hey there, reader,

If you've picked up this book, you're in for a ride—literally. Forget what you thought you knew about success stories, because Dame Sarah Storey's journey is here to flip the script.

You see, we live in a world obsessed with instant success and overnight celebs. But let me tell you, Sarah Storey isn't that kind of hero. Nope. She's the grit-and-grind, never-give-up kind of badass that the world seriously needs more of. And trust me, her story isn't just for sports fans; it's for anyone who's faced a tough spot and thought, "Is this it for me?"

Spoiler alert: It's not.

Sarah Storey's story (try saying that five times fast) is a masterclass in breaking barriers, both the ones the world puts in front of us and the ones we put in front of ourselves. It's a nudge, a push, maybe even a shove, to look at those barriers and say, "Not today."

So, go ahead. Flip the page and dive in. Whether you're an athlete, a dreamer, or just someone who loves a good underdog story, this book has something for you. It's not just about overcoming obstacles; it's about smashing through them and coming out the other side a champ.

Buckle up. You're in for an epic journey that's about way more than sports. It's about life, resilience, and the never-quit spirit that lives in all of us.

Ready to get inspired? Let's ride on!

Cheers to the journey,

S.A. Sterling

S.A. Sterling, MA

ABOUT THE AUTHOR

Meet S. A. Sterling, a storyteller on a mission to inspire hearts and minds across the globe. With a Master's Degree in Foreign Language and a passion for storytelling, S. A. Sterling embraces the beauty of communication through her multilingual skills, effortlessly connecting with people from diverse cultures.

Beyond her academic achievements lies a genuine passion for making a difference. As a devoted language teacher, S. A. Sterling empowers her students to explore new horizons and appreciate the power of words. Sterling weaves together a tapestry of inspiration which transcends language barriers and touches the hearts of many across the globe.

S. A. Sterling's thirst for knowledge and passion for personal growth extends beyond her writing desk. She is an avid reader who constantly seeks out inspiring stories that fuel her imagination and ignite her own desire to make a difference in the world. Inspired by the extraordinary journey of Dame Sarah Storey, S. A. Sterling began writing a transformative tale of triumph. Instead of simply recounting achievements, she sought to capture the essence of courage and resilience that defines Dame Sarah's life.

Through *Ride On! Dame Sarah Storey's Extraordinary Journey of Triumph: How to Unleash the Power Within, Push Boundaries, and Champion Excellence*, S. A. Sterling's heartfelt goal is to uplift and empower readers. She wishes to guide them on a journey of self-discovery in hopes that every reader will find their own courage to break free from limitations and embrace their unique path to greatness.

S. A. Sterling invites you to explore the awe-inspiring life of Dame Sarah Storey—a journey that transcends boundaries, redefines greatness, and celebrates the beauty of the human spirit.

You can connect with S. A. Sterling on social media (Twitter: @sasterling72), or visit her website (www.sasterling.com) to stay connected and explore more inspiring works.

DEDICATION

To my parents, Bruno and Gabriella, who inspire me from above — thank you for teaching me the value of hard work and dedication.

INTRODUCTION

"I've never really considered myself to have a disability," says Dame Sarah Storey (*Legend: Sarah Storey*, 2021, 0:01:13). "I've never *not* been able to do something."

In her relentless pursuit of greatness, Storey has broken records, won championships, and became an inspiration to young women worldwide. She doesn't believe in limits. She believes in pushing past them. In everything that she does, Dame Sarah Storey strives to be the epitome of greatness. Across several sports, she has defied the odds and mastered many different performance techniques to improve her skills. There are many aspects of Sarah Storey's life that are congruent with the makings of a true legend. Each chapter will peel back a different layer of her life so we may examine just how each of these formative achievements—or pitfalls—made her into the inspiration that she is today. As we look at the different challenges that Storey faced throughout her lifetime, we can learn how to overcome our toughest battles and turn them into our greatest motivators.

In this book, we'll look not just at the highlights, but at the downfalls of competing at the elite level. We'll look at the barriers that have been placed for non-able-bodied athletes, and see how Dame Sarah Storey pushed beyond them. We'll also look at how incredibly humbling her experience has been as she navigates everyday problems just like you and me. Storey has been competing internationally since she was just 14 years old. On top of being an inspiration to young women around the world, she is Britain's most decorated Paralympian, who's competed in both able-bodied and Para Sports alike. Her story is an inspiration to other young, female athletes who may feel discouraged from joining sport because of their gender, body type, or even a disability.

This story is not just about finding inspiration to be better. It's about having the courage to grow when you didn't think you could anymore. Storey didn't start competing as a cyclist until she was 28 years old. She never considered the way life would throw her off course, and yet, she still made the most out of it. You, too, can find a way to overcome any mental and physical challenge with the right mindset.

Of course, these pivotal moments in Dame Sarah Storey's life didn't come without some growing pains. It was in her darkest moments where she learned the most valuable lessons. We'll take a look at how she struggled with being bullied at a young age and what it took to overcome the eating disorder that followed suit. We will dive into the lessons that she learned from her parents, her coaches, and even her peers. Looking beyond the sport, we'll learn what some of her greatest mentors taught her. I'll even share the story of how her swim coach convinced her to give up the pool for the bike. Storey has continued to create a lasting legacy in the world of Para Sports, and we can't wait to see what she accomplishes next.

When it comes to writing about sports, it can be difficult to accurately depict the brilliance that these athletes bring to their respective fields. In an unprecedented struggle to achieve greatness, these people pour their hearts into the sport they love and leave it all out there for us to gaze upon. What's even more awe-inspiring is the stories that these athletes tell. They share the lives that they lived before the spotlight, the peaks and the pitfalls, and how these experiences shaped them into the person they are today. You don't have to be an athlete to understand the struggle to achieve under relentless pressure—not just from your friends or your family, but from yourself, too.

When it comes to Dame Sarah Storey, not a moment has gone by that she hasn't had to fight for her spot in the limelight. From birth, she's been told that her body puts her at a disadvantage. At an early age, she learned to deal with the struggles that came with having a disability. She fought a mental and physical battle day by day, yet she still came out on top each time. With the love and support of her family, and a lot of strength, Dame Sarah Storey has redefined what it means to be a great athlete.

This is a story not just of triumph and greatness, but of unconventional femininity, courage, and resilience. Sarah has paved the way for young, female athletes to rise above the traditional conventions that hold them back. Storey advocates for women—especially young girls—to join sports without worrying what other people think. She's been passed up by coaches because of her disability and turned away by her peers for not being feminine enough (Blitz, 2021).

"[We want] to enable women to have better coverage, better sponsorship opportunities, a minimum wage—which exists for the men's peloton, but not for the women's peloton—a better and more professional set-up, and more opportunity to race," said Storey.

Her journey trying to navigate two sports that are dominated not only by men, but by able-bodied athletes, has been nothing short of inspirational. Throughout this book, we will weave together an intricate tapestry of accomplishments, challenges, and invaluable life lessons that Sarah has collected over the years.

There are so many brilliant stories to look forward to in this book. Several life lessons can be learned from putting yourself in Dame Sarah Storey's shoes— the most important being the transformative power of resilience and an unwavering belief in oneself. We'll take a look at what it takes to overcome your pain, your insecurities, and the barriers that others will try to place in your way.

I'm not here to simply rehash what you can find about her in the news or any interview she's done over the years. These stories—these memories—had a lasting impact on Storey's life and her ability to achieve greatness beyond what she could have imagined as a young girl. She is paving the way for generations of female athletes as she pushes for representation, equal pay, and inclusion in sports (*Five Days to Go: Five Record-breaking Paralympians*, 2023).

Sarah Storey's journey embodies the very essence of a legend in the world of sports: a relentless spirit, unwavering determination, and a heart that knows no limits. As we embark on this inspiring voyage together, may Sarah's triumphs and challenges ignite the spark within each of us to overcome obstacles, redefine greatness, and seize the extraordinary in our own lives.

CHAPTER 1

FROM DREAMS TO GOLD: SARAH STOREY'S UNSTOPPABLE CHILDHOOD

"My parents had me playing in the garden from as soon as I could stand up," Sarah says when asked what inspired her to do sport (*Sarah's Frequently Asked Questions*, n.d.). "We have always been a very sporty family and so playing cricket, football and racquet sports was something my sister, brother and I all did from a very early age…"

GIFTED FROM THE START

As we sift through each milestone in her life, you'll realize just how *ordinary* this extraordinary woman is. And I don't mean that in a negative way. Dame Sarah Storey is a gifted athlete that has overcome so much to be where she is in life. But she is just like you and me. She has two kids, she enjoys spending time with her husband, getting dressed up in Armani with her fellow female athletes for nice events, and she even struggled with bullying at a young age. Instead of letting these things cement her life in stone, she took these qualities and turned them into motivations (Brown, 2021).

On the 26th of October, in 1977, Britain's most decorated Paralympic champion was born. Sarah Joanne Bailey was gifted in the world of sports from the moment she could stand upright. She played anything from cricket, football, and gymnastics to swimming, track and field, and even cross country. And let's not forget about her table tennis era. She couldn't just do one thing because the variety excited her. She later told interviewers that her drive to be involved in all these different sports came from a deep yearning to compete and win for her country. She just wanted to feel what it was like to stand on the rostrum and receive a medal as the national anthem played behind her. Sarah learned to swim when she was four years old, and after that, you couldn't keep her out of the water. It was swimming that provided her first opportunity to excel, and her parents encouraged her to start thinking about the Paralympics as a preteen. It slowly, and then all at once, became her identity. She began to really define herself as a swimmer (Gallacher, 2021).

Her parents lived in Manchester, England at the time, so this was where she spent a majority of her childhood. They were the real heroes, lugging Sarah back and forth from her various competitions. Her parents had their hands full driving all over the small village of Eccles, Manchester to support their daughter's dreams—not to mention also dragging along Sarah's younger brother with them. It didn't matter what sport she was playing, her family was there to show her that no matter what the outcome was, she would always have a support system. Soon after learning to swim, she earned her 10-meter badge in the pool at her primary school swim club. At age six, she received her 3,000-meter badge. By the time she was eight years old, she was the fastest swimmer in the whole school (Thurston, 2021).

All the while, she was still playing every sport she could. Sarah was always outside trying to find something new to do. She played on an adult table tennis team as part of the training for her age group events in secondary school. She was the under 13 and under 15 county champion three years in a row in Cheshire County table tennis. She was also a part of the school's netball team at the time. In fact, she admits that she could've gone on to be an internationally ranked netball player, had she not chosen to focus more on swimming at the time. But each of these sports graced her with an opportunity to showcase her different skills as an athlete. The sky was the limit, and her skills knew no bounds (Spender & Cole, 2022).

It was at Stockport Metro Swimming Club that she started getting noticed by those around her. Every Saturday, she woke up excited to go to the swimming club. She practically flew through the ranks as she passed the different qualifiers with ease. She didn't even know what the Paralympics was at the time. She was just swimming alongside her able-bodied peers like it was nothing.

Discovering the Paralympics

It wasn't until she turned 12 that Sarah realized she was at a disadvantage. Everyone else's lap times began to shorten, and hers remained stagnant. Around this time, she happened upon a television program about the Paralympic Games at home. Back in the late 80s and early 90s, there was little to no media coverage for the Paralympic Games. It was talked about here and there, and highlights were shown at the regular Olympic Games, but this was Sarah's first time ever actually seeing the sport in action. There was a woman named Clare Bishop (now Clare Cunningham) talking about her experience training for the Paralympic Games. Only she, too, had a lower arm deformity and was competing with a partially amputated arm. She was talking about being the youngest swimmer in the World Championships at age 12. This was Sarah's first time seeing another athlete like herself (*Sarah's Frequently Asked Questions*, n.d.).

Sarah went to practice the next day and asked her coach about it. Alastair Johnson, her coach at the time, encouraged her to reach out to the leader of North West Disability Swim Squad. Thanks to the hours she put in at the swimming club, and the 18-months' worth of letters that she wrote to the leader of the North West Disability Swim Squad, it wasn't long before she was personally invited to attend a regional competition. This was an opportunity for her to be selected for the National Championships, so naturally she gave it her all. In her own words, she "wiped the floor with everybody."

There, she met a woman who was involved in a higher level of British Para Sport. She sent Sarah to a training camp in Birmingham called Fox Hollies. It was a weekend-long training camp for amputees and kids with other physical disabilities. At first, she was the slowest swimmer there, but over the course of just a few days, she rose through the ranks and finished in lane six with the fastest swimmers there. She was just happy to be competing against people who were similar to her. It didn't matter if the other swimmers beat her time, because she was finally pushing herself a little harder. There was a young girl named Claudia Banks who, despite having a disability, walked around the camp with her head held high because she'd never been beaten and she held several world records. Her confidence was practically oozing out for everyone else to glare at. Banks beat Sarah, but she also gave Sarah an important lesson: You can't control what others are doing. You can only control your own actions; you can only better yourself. So she did, and she's chased this mindset throughout her entire career (Rosa, 2021).

Scouts at Fox Hollies took note of her excellence that weekend and reached out to her a few weeks later with the great news. She was asked to debut as a Paralympic swimmer in the 1992 Paralympic Games in Barcelona. She won three gold medals, two silver, and a bronze. Sarah was just 14 years old at the time, and she did all of this without a fully functioning left hand (Thurston, 2021).

"I came back from those games with six medals, and it was just something I wanted to be able to do every week," Sarah said in an interview with *Cyclist Magazine* (Spender & Cole, 2022). "I just wished that the whole games' experience was a permanent place to live."

When Sarah Storey was born, her arm was entangled in the umbilical cord. As a result, her hand did not develop as it should have, and she was left with minimal functioning in her left arm. She has a little bit of a wrist and a few of the carpal bones, but most of them are fused together now. There is a small thumb joint on the inside of her hand, but it doesn't give her the kind of grip that it should (Lloyd, 2021).

Her disability falls under the umbrella category of congenital hand deformities, which can affect any part of the hand and is present from birth. They result from injury, disease, or other complications during the birthing process. It can leave the hand simply disproportionate to the other, or there can be complete absence of bones and cartilage in the hand. There are seven types, or classifications, of congenital hand deformities that range from failure to form digits all the way down to generalized abnormalities. Treatments vary by case, and all of the factors of your individual case should be considered—including medications, procedures, or therapies—before deciding to try any cosmetic surgeries (Kagel, n.d.).

There are surgeries that can be done to increase movement of the hand, but since Sarah has limited digit formation anyway, there was no need to try and surgically unfuse the bones. Prosthetics can be used to make the patient more comfortable, but Sarah has always considered the physical deformity in her hand to be a great source of power—a demonstration of her strength of character. Her family always encouraged her to look beyond the physical differences between herself and her peers and recognize that being different is not a negative thing at all.

FAMILY: AN UNWAVERING SUPPORT SYSTEM

Sarah's dad was a lacrosse and rugby player in his day, and her mother was always equally outdoorsy. Both her parents were scout leaders as well, and they would always encourage Sarah and her younger siblings to venture outdoors in their free time rather than rotting their brains in front of a television. There was always a bit of healthy competitiveness in the household when it came to games and training for sports. Her parents just wanted them to be healthy and active. They provided a foundation in which Sarah could grow and harness her abilities. Sarah was sent to a great primary school where the head teacher, Chris Parker, was into all sports. He recognized the academic benefits of happy and healthy children and would encourage the students to every sport possible. Every student learned to swim at the school swimming club, and most afternoons were spent learning outdoors instead of enclosed behind the four walls of a bleak classroom (Spender & Cole, 2022).

A Gateway to Excellence

As I said before, there was little to no coverage of the Paralympic Games at the time, so when Sarah saw that program, and she finally saw another athlete who had a similar disability to her own, it was all she could think about. The one thing that got her up in the morning was getting to compete more and more for her country. She was set on building a name not just for herself, but for Paralympic sports in general. Her coach, Alastair Johnson, was a deaf Olympian who had moved into coaching, so he was more than happy to help Sarah pursue her dreams. At first, he was hesitant because he said he wasn't sure if she even considered herself disabled. But after a few serious conversations about competing at the Paralympic level, Johnson told her about the different classifications that went into Paralympic sport and promised to look into finding other swimmers with similar disabilities that she could compete against alongside what she was already doing with the school's swimming club (Rosa, 2021).

Around the age 15, she was finally deemed old enough to govern her own sleep schedule. She started training in the mornings before school, and she continued to dream about winning more gold medals for her country. Her parents wanted her to focus on growing up well instead of pushing herself too hard, but she couldn't help herself. Her face was already plastered all over the local newspapers, and her coaches were breathing down her neck in anticipation of a new broken record. In 1992, Sarah was the first female recipient of the Manchester Evening News Sports Personality of the Year. She even had some television coverage during the Manchester sports highlights alongside the other greats champions of the 90s like Lord Chris Holmes and Baroness Tanni Grey-Thompson (Spender & Cole, 2022). All of this before turning 16.

Everything seemed to be falling in place for her. She was in a position to not only compete for her country as she always dreamed of, but she was also opening up this grandeur world of Para Sport that would ultimately change her life forever. Finally, she would have the opportunity to boast about something that made her feel happy—something that made her feel seen. Sarah wrote to *Blue Peter*, a television program that covers pop culture, sporting events, and everything in between, before traveling to Barcelona for her Paralympic debut. She practically pleaded for the production team to start getting more coverage of the Paralympic Games so that young people—especially those who have disabilities—would get a chance to see what is possible in the world of Para Sports. They loved the idea, so when she arrived in Barcelona, a *Blue Peter* camera crew followed her around for the majority of the event, documenting her experience as a Paralympic swimmer. She was invited to the studio alongside legends like Tanni Grey-Thompson and Chris Holmes, and they all sat around and discussed the excitement around finally getting some representation for the Paralympians (Rosa, 2021).

BULLYING AND SELF-DISCOVERY

When she finally got her license, Sarah would come to school almost every day with wet hair and a damp book bag. Her entire schedule revolved around the pool. When could she get some training in? How would this affect her physique? Would she have time to swim before this prior commitment, or would she have to make time after? Everything was decided by the pool. Despite never-ending body aches and a constant runny nose, the thrill of swimming refused to leave her body, even when she started to deal with the cruelty of teenagers (Gallacher, 2021).

Sarah was bullied for not being like the other girls. They relentlessly joked about her wet hair to her face and behind her back. She recalled hiding in the stalls in the bathroom waiting for groups of girls to leave because they were snickering about her for being aloof and driven. They'd say things like "Who does she think she is, coming in here with wet hair and not talking about what she's up to? Just wait until I get a hold of her" or "Why is she never available on the weekends? She's always rushing around after school and during lunch." Their curiosity turned into cruelty quickly. She was a walking conversation stopper. They figured that Sarah thought she was "too good" to talk about the games at school or even try to make friends. Had she talked about the games, she would only have been met with more snide remarks like "big head" or "show off." It was a double-sided coin. When they didn't talk about her, they stared mercilessly as she cowered past them down the halls.

Whenever she sat down in the classrooms or at lunch, other girls would move away, or even remove chairs from their tables, leaving Sarah isolated— oftentimes she was surrounded by the boys who could care less about what was really going on. When she gave up trying and simply talked to the boys instead, the other girls would make remarks like "Look at Sarah, trying to get a boyfriend." One of the more hurtful aspects of this time was that one of Sarah's greatest tormentors started as someone close to her. Sarah told interviewers that the girl must have not liked where Sarah's career was going. Maybe she didn't like where *her own* career was going. In the end, it came from a place of ignorance. Or maybe it was jealousy. People at her school couldn't understand why she was so unique, or why she was so motivated. Why would someone choose to go train in a public swimming pool before school instead of getting as much sleep as possible? Who would rather train on the weekends than party? All Sarah could do was try to shut it all out and wait for the weekend to finally come, so she could finally be back in the one place that made her feel comfortable in her own skin: the pool (Rosa, 2021).

Eating for Your Sport

Nobody else seemed to care about planning for the future. They were too stuck in the moment, worrying about what outfit they should wear to school the next day and if their makeup was running. Even though she was doing what made her happy, Sarah started to feel alone. She became insecure with all those eyes on her all the time. The rushing around became less about training and more about avoiding these people at school. It took a toll on her mind and her body. She stopped eating at lunch time. Instead of walking to a place to eat or bringing her own lunch, she'd just take a walk around the village until her next class. This followed her home as she picked through her dinner under the watchful eyes of her family. After about a year, people on the swim team started to take notice. During the National Junior Swimming Championships, one of the other parents around the pool approached Sarah's dad and asked if Sarah had been ill over the past term. She noted that Sarah had gotten painfully thin, and that they should try to monitor her eating habits. Over the next few weeks, Sarah remained sickly thin, so her mother asked her to see a General Practitioner (otherwise known as a GP).

"You could do with a jam sandwich," said the GP after taking one look at Sarah Storey (Rosa, 2021). "Okay, Sarah. I understand that you're having a tough time, but if you don't eat, then you won't be able to compete in any sport. I need you do a food diary, and I need to see that you're eating healthily enough to be an athlete, because it's really important to me that we don't lose you... I think your eating is disordered, but I don't think you have an eating disorder."

The practitioner told Sarah that if she let this disorder get the best of her, then she'd constantly be in a state of having to support herself through an eating disorder. This was enough motivation to begin emphasizing food intake rather than focusing on the thoughts and behaviors of those around her. Sarah admitted that she didn't even like not eating, and having the food diary gave her a way to justify to herself that eating was okay. She realized she could control how much she ate that day to advance not just her health, but her career as an athlete. What she couldn't control was the cruelty and behavior of other people. Her parents echoed the urges of the GP. They told

Sarah that you can't change it if someone doesn't like you, but you can reframe your thinking around the idea. They told her that those other girls were just jealous and to focus on her swimming friends. They reminded her that her career in sport would outlast this bullying at school. To this day, she encourages other athletes to explore this mindset of "eating for their sport." A healthy diet can fuel you to be a great athlete, and it can alter your thinking by giving you a sense of control (Lloyd, 2021).

The Impact of Bullying on Female Athletes

Starving yourself is just one form of self-harm. As more and more women are entering the world of sports, psychologists have started to look at the psychological health of female athletes. Unfortunately, the negative effects of social media on female athletes is far greater than it is on male athletes. The bullying has led to an increase in disordered eating and other forms of self-harm. This has physiological effects on the female athlete, and oftentimes, it affects their ability to perform or even recover from a sports-related injury or chronic fatigue. According to a report published by the Annals of Joint, the psychology of the female athlete is unique and should be looked at in terms of resilience and subsequent coping behaviors (Herrero et al., 2021). Christina Herrero and her colleagues identified protective coping behaviors and harmful coping behaviors in hundreds of female athletes. A number of women reported struggling with eating disorders, or even sustaining sports-related injuries, as a result of bullying or other personal struggles.

Since female athletes struggle with these psychological disorders twice the rate that male athletes do, it's important for the ones who have survived those dark days to motivate young women to push forward. Talk to your teammates, especially the older ones, because they've probably gone through a lot of the same stuff you have. Teammates provide an unparalleled sense of camaraderie, and being a member of a team can positively affect your ability to cope with negative emotions. Especially in the case of eating disorders, it also gives you a chance to receive necessary intervention when your psychological disorder begins to affect your performance. Teammates, coaches, and medical staff alike should be prepared to step in and help facilitate a proper recovery process.

One of the most important tools for altering these maladaptive behaviors is to introduce practices of mindfulness. Learn to sit with yourself and process your emotions in a way that has a positive effect on your mind and body. Focus your attention on your experiences in a nonjudgmental way. Stay in the moment and self-regulate your emotions by being aware of your bodily sensations. These mindfulness practices will allow you to cope with your negative emotions when they flare up so that they don't result in a knee-jerk reaction toward self-harm (Herrero et al., 2021).

"Many people with eating disorders talk about having no control over something else," says Dame Sarah Storey, "but this [your food intake] is the thing that they can control. So, being able to control it in a positive way rather than a negative way was vital to being able to help me almost snap out of it—if you like" (Herrero et al., 2021).

Embracing Her Disability

And like I said, those bullies couldn't keep Sarah down for very long. Her passion for sports only grew in the shadows of her girlhood. She knew that sports were not a place to be comfortable, but a place where she could test her limits and grow. At the time, it seemed like something she could never escape, but in the end, the bullying only perpetuated her growth as an athlete and as a person. Sports gave her a chance to grow up quicker in a way. She learned a lot from the mentors that were available to her, whether that meant coaches and trainers or just the older swimmers on her team. In the pool, she wasn't the oddball who was too obsessed with her hobby to enjoy her childhood. There, she was exposed to the real world. She learned to put things into perspective so she could focus on races. Her teammates taught her not to tire herself out and how to avoid getting overstimulated. Swimming gave her a place to ignore all of the stressors that came with being a teenage girl. She always knew it would outlast her school days anyway (Performance People, 2023).

"[Being bullied] helped shape my identity and my career," Storey says in an interview with *The Guardian* (McRae, 2015). "Sometimes it would have been nice to fit in, but my whole goal was to compete at elite level. It wasn't great at the time, but I found ways to deal with it and I then changed to a college for my A-levels."

Changing your mindset is so essential to maintaining your health, mentally and physically. Sports are a great way to change your mindset at a young age. You have so many opportunities to look closely at those around you—the ones who aren't involved in sports—and you get to experience so much more. You grow up quickly in the world of competitive sports. Sports are more about the journey. It's about everything that surrounds the culture. Sarah loves the traveling, the meeting new people, and simply the feel of the diamond-like, glittering water on her skin as she dives into the water. There is nothing more freeing than the sensation of swimming through crystal-clear water, your heart pounding in your ears, and not a single negative thought rushing through your head.

SUPPORT SYSTEMS: THE KEY TO RESILIENCE

Sports have also given Sarah a chance to grow some thicker skin. If your competitors don't like you, or you've got a nasty coach, teammates, or trainers, then you have to learn not to react. As an athlete, these people are there to help you grow into the best version of yourself. They aren't there to coddle you, because then you'll remain stagnant right where you are now. You have to be able to regulate your emotions when you're competing, and this skill can follow you back into the classroom. Of course, it took Sarah some time for these lessons to set in, but now she urges other young girls to learn from her experiences so they don't fall into the same trap that she did. She makes it her responsibility to show other athletic girls that women don't have to come to school with fancy clothes and blow-dried hair to be happy. Sometimes, the girl who comes to school in a tracksuit with wet hair is the one on track for greatness.

"Share the turmoil you're going through with someone trusted who will listen. They may not have any advice to offer at that point. There may not be anything that can be done right at that second, but at least it's shared," says Sarah. "A problem shared is a problem halved."

Once the problem has been shared with someone else, you always have that person to turn to when things seem the most bleak. This can be a friend, a teacher, or even a parent. As long as you can recognize that you're not alone. You're on your own path to greatness at this very moment; you just don't know it yet. Like Sarah, you just need to surround yourself with a positive support system that motivates your growth instead of trying to block it. She had a few friends at school who would step in and stand up for her when they could, but they weren't always there. It was her family who had to encourage her to look for that peace inwardly instead of always looking for a way to fit in. It was time for her to start standing out. Sarah's family has been one step behind her every step of the way, and that was enough (Fuller, 2021).

The Power Behind Having Your own Fan Club

Having your own little fan club can be extremely motivating for your mental health. If you build yourself a proper support system of people, then nothing you do is accomplished alone. In the world of sports, Sarah enjoys the aspect of "who gets to go with," as in who will be in the stands supporting her this time. Her family never missed a match when she was growing up. Whether it was a gymnastics showcase, a tennis tournament, or a swimming meet, they were always there. That kind of support gave her the motivation she needed to continue on—to get past all the self-doubts, the bullying, and the mental and physical toll that sports has on the body. Nowadays, she gets to bring her own family. In an interview, she confesses that the only times she didn't have someone in the stands was during the 2011 races in Columbia and in 2012 at the South Africa road race (Gallacher, 2021).

"Make sure you have plenty of strings to your bow so you've got choices," Sarah's dad would tell her as a kid, "then you can choose what you want to do."

He was talking about support. One of the many things that has paved the way for Sarah's journey to greatness is her support systems; her bowstrings. Without support from her family, she may have never joined sports in the first place. She could have let the bullies win and never stepped foot in the pool again. She may have continued to struggle with her eating habits or given up when she started to realize that her disability *did* make her different. Without the love and support of her family, she wouldn't have realized that different doesn't mean bad. If Sarah wasn't different, she wouldn't have pushed herself to be better day by day. One of her greatest motivations is being able to show her bullies what she was working toward (Gallacher, 2021).

"The nastiest people I have not seen since 1994," Sarah says, "and I don't know where they are, and I don't profess to care either" (Performance People, 2023).

Bullying is something that exists in our society, and there isn't one fix-all method to eradicate it, so we kind of learn to deal with it when we're young. When you figure out how to navigate and work through it, Sarah believes that you should lend a hand to those who might still be struggling with that part of their life. As you go through life, you hope that people will be kind, gracious, and courteous, but oftentimes people are cruel, selfish, and relentless. The most important thing is to keep your own light alive. Don't let their darkness seep in. When faced with cruelty, smile at your tormentors, and show them you are stronger than their efforts to tear you down (Performance People, 2023).

"I was just different," says Sarah (Fuller, 2021). "And difference often gets singled out and bullied. I was just in that bracket. But I just wanted to be an athlete more than I wanted to be anything else, so I trundled on."

Going into year ten at school, Sarah was coming back from having accomplished something rather extraordinary for her age. As she worked to keep her grades up, she was also getting invites to National Awards ceremonies. Thanks to the incredible mentors and teammates she got to retreat to on the weekends at the swimming club, she was able to imagine herself in a place beyond the bullying. In her mind, she'd already experienced so much that she wasn't so focused on getting through the day anymore. Things got easier as she was more mindful about her future as an athlete. Her coaches, parents, GP, and teammates alike showed Sarah that her decisions impact more than just her day at school. With a deeper focus, Sarah excelled at school—and in the pool—until she graduated and moved on to training at an even higher level (Fuller, 2021).

LOVE, MARRIAGE, AND FAMILY

Sarah Bailey became Sarah Storey after marrying fellow Paralympic champion and cyclist Barnaby Storey. Better known as Barney Storey, her husband has been a great motivation and even a personal mentor to Sarah. They met as teammates in 2005 at a pre-Paralympic training camp in Cyprus. Over the course of the next few months, they saw more and more of each other until, ultimately, they decided to move in together. They would train together on the weekends, and spend their free time at home chatting nonstop about cycling techniques and watching sporting events. He himself is a tandem pilot coach who retired from competing in the Paralympic Games himself sometime after he won a Gold in the 1-kilometer time trial, and a Silver in the Tandem Sprint (*Barney Storey,* n.d.). They live in Disley, Cheshire with their two children, Louise Marie Storey and Charlie John Storey. With the countryside on their doorstep, the couple has plenty of opportunities to practice cycling while also spending plenty of quality time with their children, instilling the same family values that Sarah grew up with. Sarah is proud to support her children in whatever they choose to do in the future, because without that same support from her own family, she would never have been able to achieve so much in her lifetime (Cornish, 2021).

"My family is essential to everything," says Sarah in an interview with TotalWomensCycling (Stevenson, 2013). "Without my family, I couldn't do what I do."

Dame Sarah Storey has accomplished many great things in her lifetime, and she doesn't plan on slowing down anytime soon. Since 1992, Sarah has been winning gold medals, breaking records, and earning more world championships than any female Para-athlete in the world. If you thought her success as a teenager was impressive, just wait until you see all of the incredible feats Sarah has crossed and barriers she has broken through for her fellow Para-athletes and female athletes.

Dame Sarah Storey is not only the most decorated female Paralympian of all time, but she's also the most successful Paralympic athlete in the whole world. In the next chapter, we'll take a look at how she rose through the ranks at lightning speed, claiming victory at nearly every event she attended. We'll also examine how Sarah's time in the spotlight has impacted not just the realm of female athletes, but of para-athletes all across the globe.

CHAPTER 2

A PATH TO GREATNESS: RISING THROUGH THE RANKS

"Can I be sixteen again?" Sarah Storey says during an interview with a laugh (MacInnes, 2021). "I never set out on this journey to be Britain's greatest Paralympian, but to match the best man—and to have more other medals—is just a dream come true."

A CHAMPION THROUGH AND THROUGH

Just to give you an idea, Dame Sarah Storey has won seventeen gold, eight silver, and three bronze medals for Britain in the Paralympic Games. She earned five of those gold medals before even turning 20. She's also broken seventy-seven World Records, collected forty World Championship titles—making it sixty medals total from world championships. Sarah has collected over 140 National titles so far, and she currently holds twenty-one European titles (*Sarah Storey*, n.d.). She is internationally recognized as Britain's most decorated female Paralympian and is also considered the most successful Paralympic champion of all time. Sarah is celebrated as the most outstanding sportspeople of her generation. All of these accomplishments across two sports: cycling and swimming. Sarah professes that she was one of the few people who had ever successfully made that change from one sport to another so late in her career. Her incredible resilience allowed her to seamlessly transition without skipping a beat. There was no doubt in her mind she'd be able to succeed in whatever sport she committed herself to (Fuller, 2021).

As you know, Sarah began her Paralympic journey in Barcelona as a young teen in 1992. It was her first opportunity to show the world her potential. She put her whole heart into it and started her career off strong by beating Claudia Hengst—a German swimmer who was undefeated at the time. Sarah beat her not in one match, but twice, and she ended up setting a record time in the 200-meter individual medley that remained unbeaten for over 20 years. In her debut as a Para-athlete, she brought home two gold, three silver, and one bronze medal (Mercer, 2021).

Despite the difficulties that she was experiencing at school, she competed at the Paralympic Games four years later in Atlanta. There, she added another impressive tally of three gold, one silver, and a bronze medal for Britain.

Over the course of the next eight years, she brought home four more silver medals and a bronze one for her country. There were a few setbacks that Sarah says affected her performance at the Sydney Games in 2000 and the Athens Games in 2004, but she was still celebrated by her family, her coaches, and young female athletes who looked up to Sarah.

Without skipping a beat, Sarah transitioned into cycling before the 2008 Paralympics due to mental and physical complications in the pool. However, you couldn't tell she'd ever been down watching her race around the track on those performance bikes. At the 2008 Beijing Games, Sarah brought home two gold medals and a record time that placed her in the top eight at the Olympic finals. This was her very first time competing as a cyclist, yet she stood upon that rostrum alongside her husband, a celebrated Paralympic cyclist, and grinned like she always belonged up there.

In 2010, Sarah became the first Para-cyclist to compete at the Commonwealth Games against nondisabled cyclists. She placed sixth in the individual pursuit, but there was no frown on her face that day. Finally, she was given an opportunity to compete alongside her able-bodied peers like she was back to being eight years old at the school's swimming club. At the Paralympic Games in 2012, she added four more gold medals to her collection. She competed and won in both the track and road races, demonstrating once again her incredible determination to be the best at whatever she puts her mind to is all she needs to succeed.

"To me the biggest motivation is not just limited to sport," she says (Snape, 2021). "It's about the whole of your life—for me or for anyone else. I always advocate being the best you can be."

Her rise to the top wasn't slowing down either. Sarah Storey was made a dame in the 2013 New Year Honours List and she was also nominated for BBC Sports Personality of the Year. At the 2016 Paralympics in Rio, Dame Sarah Storey brought back three more gold medals for her country, officially making her Britain's most decorated Paralympian of all time. At the Rio Games, she broke her own world record while qualifying to reach the final against fellow Briton cyclists Crystal Lane-Wright (Mercer, 2021).

FIRST AND FOREMOST, A SWIMMER

Let's slow it down for a minute and take the necessary time to examine these incredible feats in more detail. Sarah is no stranger to rising quickly through the ranks. We've already discussed how quickly she flew through the different groups at her primary school's swimming club, but this was just a taste of what was to come. I think one important aspect of her growth was that she never wanted to "crush" her competition. She was always trying to break her own records, beat her own times, and expand her own knowledge of the sport. Her swim club would occasionally host galas where they would compete against one another, or sometimes a local school or two. By the time she was eight, she was the fastest swimmer around Manchester. She was undefeated, but this never affected her ability to bond with her teammates. Her swim club was her greatest escape. It was a place where she could be with like-minded individuals who pushed each other to grow, not to *change*. Their coach, Lynn Ashton, always encouraged Sarah and her teammates to try new things by exposing them to several galas, life-saving competitions, and even synchronized swimming at times.

Let's not forget that she was a three-time table tennis champion in her hometown and a renowned netball player before she committed her time fully to swimming. At this point, she was still playing alongside her able-bodied peers, never skipping a beat. It wasn't until she turned 12 that she noticed small differences in her performance compared to her friends; she wasn't quite as quick as she wanted to be. When Sarah learned about the Paralympics from that one, short television special about Clare Bishop who was training to compete in the Paralympic Games, everything changed for her. Alastair Johnson, a deaf Paralympian-turned-swimming-coach, was her coach at the time, and he was able to facilitate her transition into Para Sport. He researched events she could compete in that would allow her to swim alongside other athletes with similar disabilities, while also helping her maintain her spot on the school's team. At her first competitive Para Sport event—a regional competition that would qualify her for the national championship—she blew the other swimmers out of the water. She was sent to a training camp where she, once again, climbed through the ranks with impeccable speed. She finished in lane six with some of the fastest swimmers there. At the end of the event, she was selected to be on the British swimming team for the Paralympics (Rosa, 2021).

A Paralympic Debut That Set the Bar High

While it was a rather windy road, the destination was worth the wait. Sarah still thanks her coaches and her parents who made it possible to be involved in all these different events, which exposed her to the people that would begin advancing her career. It was hard enough for an adult at the time to learn about and then start training for the Paralympics, let alone a teenage girl. But thankfully, their presence facilitated her growth which resulted in an exceptional debt. Sarah secured six podium-ranked medals for her country— two gold, three silver, and a bronze, all before her 15th birthday. So young, and yet already, she'd collected a number of medals for her country under her belt. Now it was time to train for the next Paralympic event in 1996. At the Paralympic Games in Atlanta, you could tell that Sarah had grown more comfortable in her own skin as a swimmer. She was about to be 19 and she was a serial winner. She went into her events with her chin up and a smile on her face. To her, she was there to beat her score from four years prior. And she did just that. Sarah won three gold medals, two silver, and a bronze for Britain and returned home as the first female Paralympian of her generation to win seven gold medals as a teenager (Rosa, 2021).

Her attitude is what really made her a great champion. She had this unmatched self-determination and ability to self-reflect on her achievements. In an interview with Jeremy Snape, Sarah talks about this ability to work for her goals for her own benefit instead of an external force (2021). She doesn't do it for the prize. It isn't about the money, the flowers, or the fancy new goggles her friend's parents would hold over their children's heads to motivate them. For Sarah, she was able to find that gratification inwardly instead of searching for it in other ways. She knew that she wasn't always going to win everything, so she developed a coping mechanism in order to move forward with her head held high (2021). The problem with looking for someone else to validate your feelings of achievement is that sometimes people won't share your excitement. They won't always be there to provide the motivation that you need in order to achieve greatness. Your mindset has to be singular—focused on the goal and nothing else—or else you'll constantly be trying to measure yourself up against impossible standards. As long as you know that you put your all into it—you know that you've worked harder than anyone else out there—then you've already won in your mind.

"I think owning one's success is down to hard work," Sarah says in an interview (Snape, 2021). "You can be fabulously talented, but if you aren't prepared to work hard then it doesn't matter how talented you are because somebody will be prepared to work hard[er]... Mental strength comes from working hard, I think."

Her swim coach taught her and the other Para-athletes to go to extraordinary lengths during training, because they weren't training for something ordinary. He believed that in order to achieve the extraordinary, you have to be extraordinary. So that's how he trained them to be. It was a quest to achieve greatness not just in the pool, but in their everyday lives as well. It wasn't an easy path. Sarah couldn't cut corners. She dedicated every moment to her career as an athlete. There was this uncanny focus that nobody could shake—not her competitors, not her bullies, not even her teammates.

She swam in four different Paralympic Games as a swimmer. Over 12 years, she'd competed in events in Barcelona, Sydney, Atlanta, and Athens, not to mention the World Championships and other events she was competing at on the side. Swimming was her first experience competing at that level, and she couldn't get enough (Gallacher, 2021). Swimming was all-encompassing. She figured she was going to be a swimmer for the rest of her life. She never imagined for a second that she'd have a career as a cyclist in just a few short years.

SARAH STOREY'S SWITCH TO CYCLING

Sarah always had a clear vision of what she wanted to achieve. She never set out with a goal to be one of the only para-athletes in history to have such a successful career across two sports. She just wanted to test her own abilities and see what she could do. With the support of her loved ones—and countless hours of training in the pool—she turned her dreams into a reality.

She completed her GSEs, which are similar to the American high school qualifications. Later, she pursued her A-levels independently, which are advanced studies beyond that of the high-school level. She then went on to university in Leeds to study sports science. It was here that Sarah, unbeknownst to herself, began to transition into cycling. We'll examine this more in depth in Chapter Three, but it was here that Sarah met a swim coach who actually refused to coach her. Sarah was extremely disappointed because she'd chosen the university because of their swim team's outstanding reputation. The coach told her that he wasn't interested in training non-able-bodied athletes, and he tried to stick her in a squad that would train at odd hours during the day so he wouldn't have to interact with them. Sarah took matters into her own hands and quit the team altogether. She began training herself during the hours that worked for her, but there was a mental and physical toll on her body that couldn't be ignored for long. When she wasn't selected to go to the pre-Paralympic event in 1999, it took everything in her not to be completely crushed.

"I was the one person they left out that probably should have gone as well," said Sarah in an interview with *Driving Force* (Rosa, 2021, 00:26:59). "He said I was making it [the fatigue] up, there was nothing wrong with me. I just needed to get over the fact that I was 21 now and probably coming to the end of my swimming career. I wasn't best pleased to hear that, as you can imagine. I wanted to prove him wrong."

From 2000 until 2004, Sarah was battling a severe ear infection that would eventually keep her from the pool until it could heal properly. She told interviewers that she could have gone deaf had she not transferred her energy into finding a solution to keep swimming. Her persistence to get in the water was unmatched, though, and she tried everything from specialized earplugs to a helmet in the water. Nothing could keep water from entering her ear, and her doctors eventually told her that trying to continue swimming would only permanently damage her body further (Rosa, 2021).

While she continued to push herself both in and out of the pool by using other methods of keeping fit like cross training, kayaking, and cycling, Sarah couldn't help but consider her coach's words. Was she truly coming to the end of her swimming career? But Sarah was already cycling in her free time. As a way to stay fit, she was cycling around Leeds to and from class, completely oblivious that she was paving the way for her transition into a new Paralympic sport. While it was still one of the most difficult periods in her life, Sarah is still somewhat thankful for the events that took place. Without those barriers, she would never have even considered herself to be a cyclist. After the Games in Athens, she wanted to try something a little different and challenge herself as a cyclist. She went down to the velodrome to learn how to ride on the track. The track bike was such a different way to ride than she'd been used to. The fixed gear and lack of brakes frightened her at first, but she was confident in her abilities, and in her own resilience. She got up on that track bike and immediately fell in love. Her passion for competing seamlessly transferred to cycling, and after only a few months of training, she was eager to start competing to test her abilities.

It was during that process that the British Cycling team saw her riding around—broad shoulders and all—and they stopped Sarah in her tracks. "What are you doing at the velodrome?" they asked. "Why aren't you in the swimming pool?" She explained to them her situation, and they offered her a bit of coaching to get her started. Eventually she was sent to a time trial race in 2005 to see what kind of potential Sarah Storey could bring to the track. She competed at her first Road World Championships in 2006, where she took home two silver medals. But even as she started training for the 2008 Paralympic Games to be a cyclist, she was still trying to make swimming work. She would sneak off to the pool despite her doctor's recommendations to stay away from the water. That part of her couldn't be shed off easily (Rosa, 2021).

And yet, she went to the 2008 Paralympic Games in Beijing and proved to the world that she was one of the greatest champions. If people hadn't noticed before, she was now a force to be reckoned with. She won two gold medals—one in the C5 individual pursuit on the track, and the other in the C5 Time Trial on the road—in her very first race as a Paralympic cyclist. Her time was so impressive that it secured her a place in the top eight at the Olympic finals. At the following Paralympic Games in London, she blew her competition out of the water in both the track and the road events. She won a staggering four gold medals at the London 2012 Games, one of them being the very first gold medal for Britain in the C5 women's road cycling time trial. Of course, we'll take a closer look at why in Chapter Four: A Life

Beyond Sport, but Sarah missed the 2013 season. It was during her return to international competition in 2014 that she added twelve World Championship titles to her collection. It was a precursor event for the Rio 2016 Paralympic Games, but she treated it as she always did—as an opportunity to better herself and break her own records—and that was exactly what she did. At the 2016 Games in Rio, Dame Sarah Storey obtained three more gold medals and was officially given the title of the most successful and most decorated British female Paralympian of all time (*Dame Sarah Storey DBE*, n.d.).

She told an interviewer that she used to have these incredible vivid dreams of swimming in pools and racing against other swimmers. Now, she dreams as a cyclist, racing past others at lightning speed—her heart pounding when she wakes up. Not a lot of athletes successfully change sports so late in their career, and even less have become as successful as Sarah has after the transition. She's an inspiration to anyone who thinks it's too late in life to make a change. There is always opportunity for growth, especially if you put forth all your effort into succeeding.

Sarah laughs as she recalls a story from her wedding when one of her uncles approached her and said "I am so glad you gave up that swimming—you look so much more lady-like around your shoulders now." She boasts about this "family feel" around her career as an athlete. Her husband is now her cycling team manager, her parents have still put their all into being at each event to support their daughter, and she even has two kids of her own now who help Sarah celebrate her victories (Hickmott, 2008).

The switch to cycling may have even saved Sarah from a lot of stress, especially if you consider the toll it took on her as a teenager. That's not to say that swimming wasn't good for her—because I truly believe that without it, she wouldn't be at the level she is today—but things do happen for a reason. Her drive to succeed in whatever she put her mind to has carried her so far. And there is no doubt in my mind that Sarah's family, and their unwavering support for her dreams, are to thank for creating the hardworking, determined, and resilient young woman who is still out there breaking records today.

"I might be there competing by myself," says Sarah in the *Stripped Back Sport* podcast, "but I don't do it by myself by any stretch" (Gallacher, 2021).

Record Breaking Events

It doesn't matter how I break it down; to try and summarize Dame Sarah Storey's accomplishments into one chapter is to appear reductive. Just know that each of these stories has a rich history of literary and philosophical inspiration that can be broken down by looking a little deeper. We'll save that for Chapter Five. For now, let's take a closer look at some of Dame Sarah Storey's greatest accomplishments as a cyclist—starting with her appointment to damehood.

Sarah Storey was appointed Dame Commander of the Order of the British Empire (DBE) in 2013. She was recognized in the 2013 New Year Honours list after her incredible performance at the 2013 Paralympic Games in London. But it may surprise you to hear that she was actually recognized by the Order of the British Empire twice before this. First, she was made a Member of the Order of the British Empire in 1998—the same year that she won Sports Personality of the Year. Then, following her performance at the 2008 Beijing Games, she was appointed Officer of the Order of the British Empire (Duff, 2021). These titles continued to add to her tally of internationally recognized awards.

As far as her other achievements go, she holds over 140 national titles, seventy-three world records, twenty-four World Championship titles, twenty-one European titles, and seven World Cup titles. She's competed in some form of championship-level events every year since switching sports—only stopping once in 2013 and again in 2017 to give birth to her two beautiful children (Duff, 2021). Both times, she bounced back stronger than ever, once again showing female athletes that they truly can do anything they put their minds to. Not once has she allowed her disability to overpower her will to succeed. She's a legend on paper and in person. When you watch her compete, you can see her passion and dedication as it practically radiates from her. And every day, she gets to compete not just for her country, but for the little girl back in 1989 who watched a television program about someone who looked like her and dreamed of standing up on that rostrum day and night.

"I [also] harboured the desire to become a successful defending champion," says Sarah on the *TeamStorey* website (*Sarah Storey*, n.d.), "and deep down wanted to be one of those athletes who isn't just around for a Game or two, but had the resilience and work ethic to go to several Games."

In the 2012 Paralympic Games, Dame Sarah Storey made history by winning the C5 women's road cycling time trial, making it the first time Britain has ever won gold in this event. She was defending a title she'd won four years prior in Beijing, and she finished over a minute and a half quicker than anyone else in the Games. The athletes she'd looked up to—like Baroness Tanni Grey-Thompson and Dave Roberts—were her equals now. Her incredible victories in the C5 pursuit as well as the 500-meter time trial in the velodrome showed everyone that she was a dominating force on the bike. Her victory was practically a given less than halfway through the 16-kilometer course as she held a nearly minute lead on the rest of her competitions. Her fans lined the track near the finish line and celebrated Dame Sarah Storey's blatant victory. It would make her 10th title as a Paralympic gold medalist (Henson, 2012).

Between the Paralympic Games, Dame Sarah Storey was competing at the UCI Para-cycling World Championships all around the world. In 2012, she brought home two gold medals—one in the individual pursuit and the other in the 500-meter time trial—and a silver in the team sprint. In 2014, there were two separate World Championship events that took place. The Para-cycling Track World Championships were held in Aguascalientes, Mexico while the Para-cycling Road World Championships were held in Greenville, USA. In Mexico, she brought home two gold medals and one bronze. She defended her title of Individual Pursuit champion and gained a new title as the scratch race gold medalist. The bronze medal she received was in the 500-meter time trial. In Greenville, she walked away with two gold medals. First in the time trial and next in the road race. Nothing could slow her down. She went on to defend these titles the next year at the 2015 UCI Para-cycling World Championships in Switzerland. By the time the 2018 UCI Para-cycling World Championships were over, Sarah had added well over forty-eight different World titles as a cyclist alone (*Dame Sarah Storey DBE*, n.d.).

That doesn't even account for her years she spent as a championship swimmer. And she's still not slowing down. It's almost impossible to accurately count the successes of Dame Sarah Storey because they're so vast and widespread. Thankfully she shares her experiences openly in interviews so that others can learn from her incredible journey simply by seeing themselves in her.

The Laureus Awards

In an interview with Larry Hickmott, a journalist for *British Cycling*, Sarah says that one of her proudest moments in her career was being nominated for the Laureus Awards (2008). It ranks as one of the highest and most unexpected awards she could have had. Nominated alongside legends Darren Kenny and Esther Vergeer was just one of the many things she bragged about during the interview. It's a great platform for sporting celebrities to get together and honor each other's greatest achievements while showcasing the work of the Laureus Sport for Good Foundation.

She received an email in January 2008 that said she'd been nominated and invited to the event which would take place in St. Petersburg that February. She reread the email at least four times to make sure she understood it properly. Once she was sure she wasn't dreaming, she told her husband Barney, who was more than excited to support her at the event. Esther Vergeer ultimately won the nomination, however, it was an honor just to be nominated. The red carpet event was stunning, and it was a surreal experience that showed Sarah Storey just how much of an impact she'd already made on the world of sport (Hickmott, 2008).

ONCE A PARALYMPIC CHAMPION, ALWAYS A PARALYMPIC CHAMPION

The two most recent Paralympic Games were held in Rio and Tokyo. It was in the 2016 Rio Paralympic Games that Dame Sarah Storey cemented herself in history as one of the greatest Paralympic cyclists of all time. Sarah made history when she surpassed her idol, Tanni Grey-Thompson's record of eleven gold medals with her win in the 3-kilometer individual pursuit. In the

C5 Road Race, Storey found herself over a minute behind the lead cyclist. Without a moment of panic or hesitation, Storey made a move no rider could keep up with. She powered through to the finish line ahead of the rest for the last remaining ten kilometers. She finished in two hours, fifteen minutes and forty-two seconds—three minutes and twenty-nine seconds ahead of any of the competition. The 2016 Games marked fourteen gold medals on the tally —just two away from the world-record holder, Mike Kenny. He had no idea his position would be in jeopardy so soon (Steinberg, 2016). Winning was practically routine to Sarah at this point. She could bounce back from anything; it didn't matter if it was the flu or childbirth.

After giving birth to her son in October 2017, Sarah competed in the 2018 UCI Para-cycling Road World Championships in Maniago, Italy just eleven short months later. She still tells interviewers that her ability to return to sport after childbirth is one of her greatest demonstrations of strength and resilience. At the UCI Para-cycling Road World Championships, she won a gold medal in the time trial as well as a gold medal in the road race (*Dame Sarah Storey DBE*, n.d.). This set her up for greatness in the next Paralympic Games to come in 2020. Dame Sarah Storey's win at the 2020 Games in Tokyo marked a record-breaking seventeen gold medals for Britain in the Paralympics. She was so quick that—in terms of points—she nearly caught up to the tail end of the male cyclist race taking place on the Fuji International Speedway circuit. She went into the C5 Time Trial on Tuesday morning with the single-minded goal to beat the best athletes out there and come out on top. And she accomplished just that. This was her fourth Paralympic Games as a cyclist—and eight Paralympic Games overall—and her focus had only gotten sharper. It's all about taking it one race at a time.

"It's the race of truth," Sarah said in an interview with Paul MacInnes from *The Guardian*. "The chance to pitch yourself against yourself more than anything. See if you can pick off your competitors in the process. It has that little bit of everything. It has that race bit, that competitiveness, but also that single-mindedness that has carried me through my whole career. If you weren't single-minded when you followed that black line in the swimming pool you wouldn't last very long. That is probably why I am so suited to this event" (MacInnes, 2021).

On the very first day of the Tokyo Paralympic Games, Dame Sarah Storey beat her own world record by more than four seconds during the C5 3,000-meter individual pursuit. Opening day belonged to her. She made an amazing comeback on the Izu Velodrome, determined to keep pace with her teammate, Lane-Wright. She always talks about breaking your own personal times, even if it's just by a few paces, and that's exactly what she came to prove. By shaving off those few seconds, she continued to better herself, and will do so again at the next Paralympic Games if she's given the opportunity. Sarah says her win "took [her] by surprise, but a good surprise." She wonders when these things will stop feeling so surreal (*Tokyo Paralympics...*, 2021). Should making history ever *not* feel surreal though? I think it's this level of uncomfortability in the spotlight that pushed her to work for more and more titles. That curiosity of "will this ever feel normal?" kept her passion alive as she searched for new ways to succeed.

The Tokyo Games were unique because the world was dealing with the outbreak of the Coronavirus and all of its various strands. Lockdown was still in place, and the athletes were given a choice of whether or not they wanted to travel to Tokyo to compete amidst the chaos. Of course, Sarah was prepared for anything. All she wanted to do was figure out if she could still rise to the challenge after everything that was going on (Spender & Cole, 2022). Could she still beat her own time, break records, and win gold for her country when the last few months seemed so uncertain?

"For me, the answer was yes," Sarah says (Spender & Cole, 2022). "All of that resilience I feel I've built up over the years very much paid off for me."

Thankfully, her training wasn't affected much by the outbreak because of the individualistic nature of cycling. Sarah's heart was broken for all of the swimmers out there who struggled to find a place to train during lockdown. Swimming can sometimes appear to be a more privileged sport because of the lack of access to swimming pools around the world, and the COVID-19 pandemic only exacerbated these challenges.

At the 2020 Games in Tokyo, she recalls sleeping on beds "made out of cardboard" and making food in her room on a hot plate because the kitchen was shut down to everyone. But the cardboard beds were the least of their concerns, to be fair. They weren't even permitted to enter the Olympic

Village—the arena in which the Olympics are held. However, the "lockdown games" was just another challenge for Dame Sarah Storey to overcome so that she could be the best cyclist she could be. And the way Britain's team pulled together during those Games was incredible. While it wasn't her most pleasant experience competing at the Paralympics, it was still enough motivation to get her excited about the 2024 Paralympic Games in Paris (Spender & Cole, 2022).

While preparing for the 2024 Games in Paris, Sarah was involved in a horrendous crash which left her wondering if she'd ever hop back on the bike again.

"You always hope there's not going to be a crash that makes a [retirement] decision for you," said Sarah in an interview with *SportsBeat* (Harle, 2023).

But, while still recovering from a punctured lung, and nursing a number of broken ribs, Dame Sarah Storey still competed in the 2023 UCI Para-cycling World Championships and won her 42nd World Title in the time trial race. In fact, she even finished over a minute before all her competitors (Parker, 2023).

Different Classifications Explained

If you're not very keen in the world of cycling, especially in the realm of Para Sports, then you may not know what these different classifications are. First of all, when you begin training as a Paralympic athlete, there are several different classifications that will be used to classify your impairment to ensure you're competing with people at the same level as you. Types of impairments that are recognized by the International Paralympic Committee as eligible to compete in Para-cycling are as follows: impaired muscle power, athetosis, impaired passive range of movement, hypertonic, limb deficiency, visual impairments, ataxia, and leg length difference (*Classification in Para Cycling*, n.d.).

Athletes who are able to use a standard bicycle with little to no modifications compete in five different sports classes labeled C1–C5. The numbers increase with the severity of the limitation. This can be in lower and upper limbs. Those with visual impairments race on a tandem cycle with a sighted cycler in the front leading. There are trickling events which are divided into two classes: T1 and T2. T1 athletes have more significant coordination impairments than T2 athletes. Finally, there are different classes for the sport of handcycling that are ranked H1 through H5. The lower numbers indicate restrictions in both lower and upper limbs while the higher numbers indicate lower limb restrictions only (*Classification in Para Cycling*, n.d.).

As far as the different events that Sarah competes in as a para-cyclist, you've got road events and track racing events. Road events, as you can probably guess from the name, take place on the road alongside traffic, or more often, on a designated road track. Some of the more popular events include the time trial, the hill climb, and the road race. Time trials can be done individually or in small teams. Each person sets off to complete their fastest time over a certain measured distance. This typically takes place on public roads and can range anywhere from ten miles to one hundred miles. The hill climb is also exactly how it sounds: uphill. Each cyclist will climb about a mile or two up a hill for the fastest time. For the road race, a large group of cyclists will start on a private or public road and complete their circuit, which are oftentimes in a town or city center. These races can be anywhere from a few kilometers to over 200 kilometers, and the winner is whoever crosses the designated finish line first.

Track events are a bit different because the environment never changes. You'll always be competing on a velodrome during track events. The cycles are also fixed in these races to a certain gear with no brakes. The time trial is similar in track racing, only these events are typically only a kilometer long. The pursuit is a form of time trial where people compete in pairs who start on opposite sides of the track. The competition is run on a knock-out basis. A scratch race goes on for several laps, and the winner is decided by whomever crosses the finish line first. This means that if you get lapped, then that person is probably going to hold an advantage over you for the rest of the race. These are usually somewhere around fifteen kilometers long (Kidd, 2013).

EVERYTHING HAPPENS FOR A REASON

Sarah fell in love with cycling. It made the transition from her first passion, swimming, to another sport she'd never even considered before just a little easier. Sarah has always worked to improve her skills so that she can be a better version of herself. She looks at her so-called failures as motivations. When her doctor practically forced her to consider the end of her swimming career so that she wouldn't go deaf, she could have given up. But instead, she continued to stay in shape using different sports, and eventually discovered her affinity to cycling. Every challenge is an opportunity to grow, and the challenge of learning about a new sport excites Sarah. She doesn't get embarrassed easily, and she tries to help other female athletes harness this same mindset.

"You may have done it in the wrong way today," Sarah says (Spender & Cole, 2022). "But that's just the wrong way for today. Doing it differently next time will produce a different result. It always will, whether you won or lost the day before."

She met her husband—Barney Storey—during this rocky transition period between sports. They'd pass each other at the gym while Sarah was trying to figure out the basics of cycling technique. He was even one of the people who encouraged her to try cycling on the track. He'd been watching her cross train during her down time out of the pool, and he, too, could see the potential behind Sarah's athleticism. During such a stressful time of traveling to and from the doctor only to hear bad news time after time, cycling was her light in the dark. Eventually, her competitive soul drove her to start competing as a cyclist on the track and the road (Spender & Cole, 2022).

Barney was just one of the many people who helped Sarah come out triumphant over the tragedies in her lifetime. As I said before, having a support system is so valuable. This is especially true for athletes who are constantly partaking in a mental battle of "will I be better than I was last time?" Chances are, you won't always be better than you were last time. Sarah has made it her mission to help other para-athletes—as well as other female athletes—understand that your greatest competitor will always be yourself. You're going to be your harshest critic, so you also need to be your own greatest motivator. And when things get tough, look around you and ask for help from your support system.

In the next chapter, we'll take a look at some of the hardest challenges that Dame Sarah Storey had to face throughout her career. Along with what it took to rise through the ranks as a para-athlete, we'll look closer at the effects of mental health challenges, the ear infection that ended her swimming career, and even Sarah's ability to return to cycling after two separate childbirths. Do you think you could return to an elite-level competition only a few months after delivering a baby by an emergency cesarean? I didn't think so.

CHAPTER 3
EMBRACING ADVERSITY:
TRIUMPH OVER CHALLENGES

"It's okay to make mistakes—the whole journey is a process," Sarah says (Spender & Cole, 2022). "I also talk a lot about the joy of the journey. You're not trying to get to a destination, you're trying to enjoy the path of becoming a better version of yourself. Whether that's in sport, in studying, working, or even in your personal life."

THE TRANSFORMATIVE POWER OF CHALLENGES

t's important to look at this concept of "disability" not in terms of *disadvantage*, but as an opportunity to transform the way you view success. Your biggest competitor will be your own body. Whether you let it beat you, or motivate you to work harder, is up to you. Dame Sarah Storey never felt that only having one fully functioning hand would stop her. Overall, her left arm is nearly eighteen centimeters shorter than her right (*Sarah Storey*, n.d.). It didn't stop her family from motivating her to do whatever she wanted with her future.

She didn't recognize that her disability was actually her first challenge to overcome until she was a teenager. Before that, she was out playing netball with one arm, table tennis, and racketball, all without giving it a second thought that she was somehow different from her peers. She excelled in everything she tried, which only gave her more confidence to seek out the next challenge (Spender & Cole, 2022).

She really began to take notice of this first challenge at the swim club when her teammates slowly started getting faster while she seemed to be falling behind. She was just missing out on national age-group qualifying times, and the pressure started to set in. It took a while for her to realize what was happening. Since there was so little media coverage on para-athletes, Sarah had no idea that there were competitions out there that included people who looked like her. On that fateful night in 1989, when Sarah happened upon that television program of Clare Bishop, an athlete that Sarah could picture herself in, her whole world was turned around. Now, her entire focus was on getting involved with Paralympics and training alongside other para-athletes.

When she was given the opportunity to prove herself alongside other para-athletes, she absolutely excelled. Her confidence soared as she walked around the 1990 National Championships gala with her head held high. When she was invited to Fox Hollies training boot camp for a weekend, there were new challenges to face. Now that she was swimming alongside other para-athletes at the elite level, she was no longer the best in the room. In fact, Sarah admits she was one of the slowest swimmers there on the first day. But it took one weekend of receiving the proper training—and meeting some truly inspirational mentors along the way—to change Sarah Storey into the champion she would become. She was so young, and lucky to have been given the chances she had. But she was working harder than most other kids around her to get there. She governed her own sleep schedule, her food intake, and she kept up her grades in school. Sarah was even in charge of waking her parents up to make it to morning training on time and reminding them when she needed to be at training afterward. Every decision she made was done so with her future in mind.

Everyone at Fox Hollies wanted to know who she was. They could tell she was going to be the next big thing. They admired her drive, and they envied her dedication. From morning to night, Sarah was in and out of the pool trying to improve her technique, learn a new skill, or harness her inner strength so she could push just a little bit harder every time. Ten months after that weekend at Fox Hollies, she was invited to join the British swimming team, and she formally began training for the 1992 Paralympic Games in Barcelona. When the 1992 Games rolled around, Sarah had turned 14, and was one of the youngest athletes there. While she wasn't the only one her age, you could tell that people were a little more curious about her abilities. Her teammates and competitors alike watched her like a hawk during her events, but this didn't faze her one bit. As you know, she brought home five medals from the Barcelona Paralympic Games. She was at the top of her sport. Nobody could get her down. Sarah was an unstoppable force on a race with no one but herself to be the best she could be. Well, except having to return back to school in the spring (Rosa, 2021).

From Setbacks to Strength: Embracing Change and Redefining Your Limits

But all this glory seemed to fizzle away when Sarah had to return to school after those first games. There was this quiet understanding that the next

Paralympics wouldn't take place for another four years, and she'd have to return to life as normal for a little while. She tried to return to school as normal, but her reality—and her focus—had shifted dramatically, so it was hard to just "fit in." She would come to school with wet hair from training in the mornings, and she'd rush home to get ready for afternoon training. During lunch, she'd occasionally jog with the cross country team to get a little more exercise in. To her peers, she was aloof, but to Sarah, she finally understood the concept of dedication (Rosa, 2021).

"I had a bit of a problem with my year group and my classmates, who thought that because I wasn't talking about it [the Paralympics], I was too good to talk about it," Sarah says in an interview with *Driving Force* (Rosa, 2021). "It was funny because if I had been constantly talking about the Games and how good they were, then I would have been called a big head anyway."

Bullying is wicked that way. Even though she was finally finding her place in the world, there were people ready to stand in the way and make it difficult in any way they could. Her tormentors would harass her at school for not taking time to dry her hair before coming to school. They'd talk about her in the bathrooms, without a care in the world if she were listening from inside one of the stalls. The attention she was receiving in her sport seemed to be having a negative effect on her social life. The "nit-picky stuff" turned into deliberate actions of cruelty as girls would move chairs in the classrooms so she couldn't sit down. When she told her parents, they told her to be as pragmatic as she could be. There was a sensible way of dealing with their behavior, and that was by recognizing that you can't control it.

It took a very long time for this lesson to settle in, though. Sarah struggled with bullying for months before her parents even realized the physical toll it was taking on her body. When Sarah stopped eating, it nearly put her swimming career on hold. She found solace with her swimming friends outside of school, but there wasn't enough time in the pool to make up for the hours she had to dedicate to ignoring her bullies. She didn't eat in the mornings because of training, and she found no peace during school hours. At lunch, she'd sneak off and walk around the village if the cross country team wasn't practicing just to avoid the bullies in the cafeteria. When she got home, she'd pick through dinner and tell her parents she had a big lunch (Rosa, 2021).

At the National Junior Swimming Championships in 1993, one of the other parents approached Sarah's dad about her body weight. She'd gotten significantly smaller over the winter break, and a lot of people were concerned she had been ill. Sarah's dad was appalled that he didn't see this change sooner. It happened right under his nose in the shadows of their home. Sarah's mother urged her to seek help from the GP. It was more important that her daughter was healthy than if she could compete. They were worried that she'd reached a point where her food intake needed to be specially monitored.

Thankfully, Sarah pulled herself back from that edge before she could fall in too deep. Her doctor said that he believed Sarah's eating was "disordered," but she didn't yet have an eating disorder. This was great news, but it was still a new challenge for Sarah to overcome. It began with a food diary, which was recommended by her GP. Just like with training, every chance that Sarah had to eat, she did so with good intention. She reframed the way that she thought about control when it came to food intake. Instead of controlling it in a negative way, she realized that if she controlled it in a positive way, it would improve her health and even advance her skills in the pool. Eating for her sport was her way of transforming yet another challenge into an opportunity to learn.

"To be honest," Sarah says, "I didn't like not eating and this tussle I was having" (Rosa, 2021, 00:22:55).

When she wasn't eating, it was like she was giving her tormentors exactly what they wanted. She knew deep down that sports would outlast school, so it shouldn't have really mattered in the long run, but those kinds of realizations are hard to have in the moment. Sometimes it takes several years for people to recognize the strength in their hardship. And it takes even longer to see the bigger picture. However, if you take the time to give the future you a chance, you'll realize that your darkest days will come to an end. Better days will come. You can't control the behavior of other people, but you can control how you react to it. When you let other people's word and behavior hold power over you, then you're only limiting your own potential. If Sarah had listened to her bullies all those years ago, she would have never gone on to win five gold medals at two separate Paralympic events, all before the age of 20.

"When you feel like you're labeled as something, then you behave more in that way," says Sarah in the *Driving Force* interview (Rosa, 2021). "Nobody wants to behave badly. You just want to feel included and feel settled."

Adversity's Unforeseen Gifts: Uncovering the Silver Lining

When Sarah finally finished her schooling and went on to university in Leeds, she began to face a different set of challenges that she wasn't prepared for. She had carefully selected a university with a renowned swimming club in the local town so that she could continue to advance her skills as an athlete. When she approached the coach at the time, he told her that he had no interest in training "disabled athletes." And he wasn't changing his mind. She was put on a team of swimmers who didn't even want to be there. They would train at the weirdest hours during the day, and none of these times would line up with Sarah's schedule at school. They wanted her there at five in the morning and nine at night. The hours weren't healthy for someone who was trying to maximize their health to be at the top of their performance. Eventually, she quit the swim club altogether and chose to be her own coach (Rosa, 2021).

She talked to the owners of the swimming pool and was able to negotiate her own hours at the pool where she would have her own lane to practice in. Sarah finally had control over her own schedule, and she fit swimming in between school and studying in a way that worked for her. It was the only way she could get enough training hours in. Her schedule was completely maxed out every week. There was no time for hanging out with her roommates, going out on dates, or even attending the occasional college party. But her roommates didn't share this same discipline. They would invite people over all hours of the night. There were parties practically every weekend, and they were always loud. Sarah was beginning to lose her mind with all the nonstop chaos.

Sarah eventually moved back home with her parents and commuted to and from school for classes only. She wasn't concerned with showing any team spirit; she didn't attend a single school sporting event. She was there to get her degree and get out. Meanwhile, she still had to maintain her physique and her swimming technique in order to qualify for the next Paralympic Games. She admits that she was piling on too much—she just wasn't sure how to properly plan the cycles of training. This resulted in a sluggishness that Sarah just could not shake. Maybe it was too much time in the car, or the stress of maintaining a training schedule, sleep schedule, and school schedule all at once, but Sarah was tired. She tried to ignore the fatigue. She pushed it off and mistook it for a dip in her talents. She pushed herself even harder to make up for these downfalls, and with no one around to regulate this behavior, she was eventually diagnosed with chronic fatigue syndrome in the end of 1998.

There were times during this period that she couldn't even walk up a flight of stairs. She was so fatigued that it began to affect her inner ears. She couldn't get through a proper warm-up, and making it down the lane in the pool was an impossible feat. She was dizzy, exhausted, and defeated. She sought help from the British Olympic Medical Center at Northwick Park, who ordered that she rest for six weeks with no training so that she would be better prepared for the Games in Sydney. During this time, people tried to discourage her, telling her that this was just the end of her swimming career coming to pass. The person in charge of the British swim team at the time told her that she just wasn't good enough anymore. He thought she was making it all up. He told her to be ready to hang her swimming cap up, and proceeded to the pre-Paralympic trial in 1999 with the best swimmers on the team—and this time, this didn't include Sarah Storey (Rosa, 2021).

"Ultimately, as an athlete, you have to accept you are not going to win all the time," Sarah says on the *TeamStorey* website (*Sarah Storey*, n.d.), "if you are producing your own personal best but still get beaten, you have done everything you could and there is nothing else you can do until the next time."

Sarah did, however, go on to compete as a swimmer in the 2000 Paralympic Games in Sydney, bringing home two silver medals for Britain. She did a watered down version of her program—four events instead of eight—and then went on to prepare for the Commonwealth Games. At the end of 2002, three months after the Commonwealth Games, she went on to win three World Championship titles.

She was back at the top of her game, ready to compete at the 2004 Paralympics in Athens when the unthinkable happened. Her mother was diagnosed with cancer earlier that same July, and she was scheduled to begin chemotherapy and a surgery for a mastectomy. Her mother actually delayed her chemotherapy and the surgery so that she could attend the 2004 Games without any complications. This was another example of just how important Sarah's support group was to her, and how deeply they cared about Sarah's well-being during any competition. The challenges didn't stop there either. Sarah picked up a flu virus in Athens that would set her back once again in terms of fatigue. She felt like she was pedaling backward toward chronic fatigue, but she was happy to hear that it was only a virus. Sarah pushed through her fatigue and brought back two silver medals and a bronze for Britain that year.

"They weren't the gold medals that I thought I was capable of," Sarah tells interviewers, "and I definitely felt like I underperformed at that particular event" (Rosa, 2021, 00:28:23).

But this wasn't the end of Sarah's story. Her unwavering determination practically possessed her over the next few years. She came down with a serious ear infection in 2005, which made it hard to train in the pool. She tried everything to keep up her hours, from ear plugs to helmets, but water just kept seeping in and exacerbating the issue at hand. Over the course of just a few weeks, she'd contracted six ear infections as they migrated from one ear to the other. She found ways to remain active outside of the pool like kayaking, running, and cycling, but the water kept calling to her. It wasn't until she'd nearly gone deaf that she finally made the choice to pull back from swimming (Rosa, 2021). But by this time, cycling had already snuck up on her.

RISING FROM THE ASHES

Sarah claims she was "too impatient" during her ear infection, and that was what led to her decision to start racing on the bike, but we know she's just being modest. Not being able to train full-time and commit herself to swimming was absolutely crushing her inside, so she had to seek that extra push somewhere else. Training on the velodrome slowly turned into competing against other athletes at the gym. She tells interviewers, Ben and Georgie from *Performance People*, that she didn't know she had what it took to be a Paralympic cyclist in those moments. She says she felt "wobbly" the first time she took the track bike on the velodrome, like "a duck out of water" (Performance People, 2023).

Everyone could see what was going on except her. Even her now-husband, Barney, urged her to make the switch from swimming to cycling after just a few short months. He was infatuated by her drive, which only brought them closer together as they became each other's greatest motivators. There are a lot of technical aspects that go into cycling. Since there are two different environments that you can compete in, you have to learn a plethora of different techniques to prepare for the worst case scenario. Naturally, Sarah wanted to compete in both track and road races. She wanted to be the best she could be, and so she used all the resources around her to hit that learning curve running.

Her swimming career had taught her everything she needed to know about the importance of having a core team. When she first began the transition from the pool to the velodrome, her core team practically flocked to her. Paul West taught her how to ride the performance bikes on the indoor track, and Marshall Thomas taught her how to master the single-gear-with-no-brakes aspect of riding on the velodrome. They introduced her to Gary Brickley who would soon become her cycling coach for years to come. There is a certain level of comfort that comes into play when you trust someone to guide you in these ways. Over time, people have come and gone from the Storey team, but overall she's been lucky to keep some of the most important people who have facilitated her growth as an athlete. In fact, she still works with the man who made her very first set of handlebars to this day (Spender & Cole, 2022).

"Continually you return to them [your network] because you know and trust that their judgment is going to be exactly right," Sarah says in an interview with *Cyclist Magazine* (Spender & Cole, 2022). "There's no, kind of, flowers around it. It's just dead, straight analysis that you need to hear."

In the summer of 2005, Sarah Storey was invited to compete in a time trial race in Belgium to see if she had what it took to start training for the 2008 Paralympic Games in Beijing. It was quite daunting for her to switch into a sport where her competitors could crash into her if they weren't careful. Sarah found it a little frightening at first to compete so closely to the handlebars of the cyclists next to her.

"I had none of the skills that were needed," said Sarah in an interview with *Performance People* (2023). "The only skill I had was my strength and my engine, so I did a lot of chasing that day."

Regardless, she impressed the British cycling team so much that she began a fast-track version of training to prepare her for the next Games—this time, in a whole new sport. She blames it on her "successive survival," but nobody on the Storey team doubted for a second that she wouldn't finish her first race. Her drive had always been unmatched, so everyone watched in anticipation as she finished with some of the fastest cyclists there. Like a phoenix, she was reborn from the ashes of her swimming career as a cyclist—and a damn good one, too. She recalls staying up late at night watching every video she could find on the Tour de France (Rosa, 2021).

There wasn't a lot of time for relaxing during these first couple of years. Barney and Sarah would stay up late at night comparing her stats and figures, comparing them to her competitors and her greatest inspirations. Sarah would have a million questions to ask Barney the moment they sat down at home, so she could perfect her own technique in areas like pedaling efficiency. There was lab testing, regular training bouts, and long discussions about how Sarah could improve her skills. To some people, it may seem like an odd relationship-to-career balance, but for two Paralympic gold medalists, this was just how things were done. It's not like the romance wasn't there—because it was—but for them, that wasn't important. What was important was that they understood one another. They admired each other for being so motivated, driven, and especially for being so supportive (Performance People, 2023).

It all progressed pretty fast. She was determined not to let an ear infection put her out of sport for good. Her time out of the water was indefinite—solely dependent on her recovery—but she was not ready to give up challenging herself just yet. Just like with bullying, Sarah had to realize that this was out of her control. The only thing she could control was trying to get better and come back even stronger. So that was where all of her effort went.

"I feel proud to have been able to say I was swimming personal best times right up to the end of my swimming career," says Sarah on the *TeamStorey* website (*Sarah Storey*, n.d.), "and even at my retirement swim meet in November 2005–I almost broke the world record over 100m freestyle, despite spending much of that year out of the water with ear infections!"

Empowerment Through Resilience: A Champion's Journey Through Struggle

Just three weeks after her first time trial as a cyclist, an invitation to compete in the European Championships landed in her lap. It was a whirlwind of "cramming" as Sarah felt the urge to fill herself up with all of the cycling knowledge she could possibly carry. She studied the sport, she asked questions, and she trained harder than she ever had before. She won the individual pursuit on the track and then went outside and won the road race, too. Sarah even broke a world record that day in addition to bringing home those first place medals (Rosa, 2021). To complicate things even more, she was invited to join both the British swimming program and the cycling program in 2006. It was up to her to decide if she wanted to return to the water and finish what she'd started, or if she wanted to embark on this new journey and challenge herself a bit more. Ultimately, it was her success in cycling that made her want to see what she was capable of. In one of her very first National Cycling Championships, she finished in seventh place in the 3,000 meter road race. Her time was just under four minutes—and not to mention she was competing against able-bodied cyclists. Never before had she finished so high up with her able-bodied peers, so she wanted to see just how far she could take it (*Sarah Storey*, n.d.).

What, then, constitutes the mentality of a champion? For Sarah, it is not just about athletic prowess, but emotional intelligence. Learning how to manage one's emotions and perspectives isn't just a skill. It's a transferable life philosophy. Sarah has learned that the only person's actions that can affect her life are her own. She has the unique ability to think about her future instead of focusing on what was, or what could have been. Sarah sets a goal and then does everything in her power to achieve it. A lot can be learned from this kind of mindset. In an interview with *Sporting Edge*, Sarah pinpointed the genesis of her mental toughness.

"I think mental toughness starts with resilience and the ability to take the rough with the smooth," Sarah says (Snape, 2021). "You won't win everything—you shouldn't win everything—but how much can you deflect the failures, or the perceived failures? How much do you let things bother you? How much do you bog down on the things you should've done rather than what you did well? What sort of resilience do you have in the world outside that's all attempting to beat you?"

The world has thrown one curveball after the other at Dame Sarah Storey, and yet, she still manages to come out on top every time. She takes every hit with her head held high because she knows it's just another opportunity to better herself. She told *Sporting Edge* that she raced in the World Championships in 2007 with a broken collarbone. She had gotten into a pretty bad crash on the bike, but thankfully she didn't sustain any other big injuries. This was just a few months before her debut as a Paralympic cyclist in the 2008 Games, and she felt that if she didn't compete in the UCI Para-cycling Track World Championships in March of 2007, then she wasn't truly prepared to compete in the 2008 Paralympic Games the following September. A broken collarbone was just another outside source trying to bog Sarah down, and there was no way she was going to let something so trivial keep her from competing.

"Mentally there was no question that I could do it," she said to *Driving Force* interviewer, Jeremy Snape (2021, 00:26:37). "I just had to figure out a mechanical way of getting around the fact that I couldn't use my left arm. Which, you know, was just a circumstance."

Once again, the world tried to throw out a barrier to block her rise to the top, and Sarah dodged it with ease thanks to her immense strength and that glimmer of determination in her eyes. She shrugged off a broken collarbone like it was nothing, and still won two gold medals and broke a world record like it was just any other competition. That same year, while still recovering from the crash, she and Barney Storey got married, and one more person was added to the Sarah Storey fan club. Her and Barney's relationship was unique because—at least at first—he wasn't out in the stands, supporting her from a distance. He was right there beside her in the heat of it, juggling his own path to greatness while he helped lift Sarah up alongside him. In 2008, they both won gold medals on the same day and stood arm in arm, showing off their medals for the photographers (Mercer, 2021).

"She's constantly driving—constantly trying to be the best person she can be —you know, in all kinds of forms of life," says Barney Storey in an interview with *Driving Force* (Rosa, 2021). "I think that kind of relentless drive that she's got is one of the reasons she's here and still competing all those years after she first started in the Games in Barcelona."

Barney uses the word "relentless" a lot when describing his wife. In her pursuit to greatness, she hasn't slowed down once. Every night it's "how can we improve this aspect?" or "what can I do differently to change the game?" Barney says he admires the drive though, and he understands her mindset as an athlete. She has a tendency to focus on the attention to detail in everything she does. When it came to shifting her focus on cycling, that attention to detail helped her refine the raw talent she already possessed. As Sarah got deeper into the world of cycling and began learning about the plethora of different events that she could compete in, it could have gotten too overwhelming had she not been able to simply look up and ask her husband for advice. That's not to say she wouldn't have figured it out eventually—because we all know she would have—but having Barney in her support system did propel her forward a bit faster than if she'd tried to train on her own again (Performance People, 2023). Who knows, maybe she would have fallen victim to chronic fatigue once again had she tried to push herself more than she could handle.

When Sarah was selected to compete for the Great Britain team that rode in the 2011 Manchester World Cup, she was elated just to get the invite. Her only concern was trying to be the best she could be and to race at the highest level she could. She jumped at the opportunity to ride at the World Cup. She won two golds—one in the C5 Road Race and the other in the C5 Time Trial (Cosgrove, 2011). To Sarah, she was riding this high that no one could knock her off. But little did she know that more heartache was just around the corner. After her success in the World Cup, she was widely tipped to be a favorite selection for the World Championships team traveling to Apeldorn.

Sarah, however, was not selected, which gutted her. Despite understanding the reasons behind her non-selection, the setback delivered a blow to her confidence. You see, she was taken away from training for some time in order to participate in the Para-cycling Track Worlds, so she missed out on vital team preparation moments (*Sarah Storey*, n.d.).

"It's important to look at the bigger picture in team selections and just something as an individual you have to take on the chin," Sarah says on the TeamStorey website (*Sarah Storey*, n.d.). "Everyone wants the team to go fast and they won the World title, so it's a huge confidence boost to everyone. The strength in depth we have in women's team pursuit in the UK is really quite superb so that will always create difficult selection choices."

Her name was dropped from the Team Pursuit squad that was going to compete in the European Championships that same year, despite meeting all the targets and producing more and more power each training session. She believes that the "right decisions were made when it mattered," but it was still another blow to her ego. Instead of focusing on the negatives, she used this time to prepare for the 2012 Paralympics. To this day, she refers to the 2012 Games as the best competition she's been a part of. Being on her home turf brought a different level of competitiveness to the track. She also had her amazing fan club in the stands—everyone from her family, Barney's family, and everyone in between was in attendance (*Sarah Storey*, n.d.).

Reflecting on the extraordinary atmosphere, Sarah described the London crowds as just *incredible*. The roar of the audience and their "generosity of spirit," as she calls it, created an electric environment where every cheer reverberated as a personal acknowledgement.

"It was an amazing place to compete," she says, "and when you won a Gold medal it did make you feel like the most powerful person in the arena, because all eyes were on you and you could wave at one person and everyone in the stand waved back!" (*Sarah's Frequently Asked Questions*, n.d.).

Navigating the Unknown: Harnessing Your Strength to Overcome

Childbirth and raising children is no easy feat. It's a daunting task in its own right, but Sarah wants to show other female athletes that with the right mindset—and a good support system—it's just another way to push you to that next level. In fact, Sarah broke the world record for the first time when her daughter was just nine months old. There have been so many terrific careers put on pause for children, and if that's what works best for you and it's what you choose, then that's amazing. But Sarah urges women to stay active if they can. Another common issue is the lack of faith coaches have in the female athlete's ability to bounce back. Of course, sometimes there are injuries that result from childbirth that may make it hard to return, but sometimes they bounce back even stronger. Sarah is just one example of why we shouldn't tell female athletes not to have kids before the end of their career (Rosa, 2021).

"I'd done anything I'd ever wanted and more, so having Louisa was the next big thing for us," Sarah says in an interview with Aimee Fuller (2021). "[But] if I came back, it was a huge bonus."

There aren't many women who have children and come back to sport. Some athletes that come to mind are Tanni Grey-Thompson, Hellen Glover, and Eilish McColgan. Inspired by some of her greatest inspirations as well as her peers, Sarah was ready for the next stage in her life. She gave birth to Louisa in the summer of 2013, and just nine months later, she was back on the velodrome training for the World Championships in 2014. In fact, she tells interviewers that she came back faster, and more eager to win than before.

Nyree Kindred used to tell interviewers the same thing after she gave birth just 13 months before the 2012 Games in London. She said there was an intense endurance spike that she'd never experienced before (Fuller, 2021). Research has shown that motherhood may actually prepare women to be better athletes in the long run. First, after childbirth, the female body experiences a spike in oxygen and blood flow. Their bodies produce more red blood cells during pregnancy, so oxygen flows more freely. A study done in 1991 proved that women can experience as much as 7% increase in oxygen efficiency eight months after giving birth. Along with the boost in oxygen comes an increase in certain hormones that support the body's recovery process—like androgen and testosterone. And let's not forget about the mental toughness that comes with giving birth. The birthing process alone would raise anyone's tolerance to pain, not to mention the several months of pregnancy-related pains that come with carrying a baby to term (Rossmeier, 2009).

So rather than viewing childbirth as a setback, it should be seen as a motivator—and that's exactly how Sarah thought about it. She even had her handlebars adjusted to accommodate her baby bump. Louisa was born June 30, 2013, and just six short weeks later, Sarah was back on the bike racing. She said it would have been sooner, but her daughter was actually born via emergency Cesarean section. The recovery process was grueling, but she didn't want to take any risks since she still planned to compete in the 2016 Paralympic Games (Lee, 2013).

"It helped that I'm very fit," Sarah says in an interview with *Express* (Lee, 2013). "However, I think it's a good idea for all new mums to get back to exercise quite soon after giving birth. It helps with recovery and mood after the stress of pregnancy."

She quite enjoyed the balance of sport life and mom life. When she competed at the 2016 Games in Rio, she rented a flat across the street from the velodrome she was competing at. After long hours of training, Sarah got to bring her daughter down to the playground in the Olympic Village and spend quality time with her family. She was even still breast feeding between training and competing in Rio. You can have all the physical support, mechanical support, and technical support in the world, but without that emotional support, it would have been difficult to bounce back as quickly as she did (Rosa, 2021).

Charlie was a little bigger of a baby, so when he was born on October 14th, 2017, Sarah knew she was going to take it easy for a little before jumping straight back into training (Fuller, 2021). Thanks to all the support she got from her family, and even her racing team, she was able to bounce back in no time (once again) and compete in the 2018 UCI Para-cycling Road World Championships in Italy where she won two gold medals in the time trial and the road race (*Dame Sarah Storey DBE*, n.d.).

Sarah says that seeing her sporting career through her kids' eyes has only motivated her to work harder. Now that they've joined the Storey fan club, Sarah has the privilege of not only continuing to do what makes her happy, but of getting to expose her children to all these unique experiences—

showing them daily that they can be whatever they want to be if they put in the hard work. Barney retired from sports just before Louisa was born, and now he is a full-time dad and the leader of the Sarah Storey Team. He makes sure that Sarah is at the top of her game both on the track and at home. With his support, Sarah's been able to breastfeed both children until they were ready to wean themselves off. In fact, she was finding time to do so during the 2014 and 2020 Paralympic Games. When they're home, they live just a couple hundred meters from her parents, who are also always there to help when Sarah needs it (Gallacher, 2021).

"With sport, because the kids are there, and they experience it in a way that sort of really drives me on even more, that kind of makes the hard work even more worthwhile," says Sarah in an interview with Kristy Gallacher (2021).

INSPIRING THE WORLD: CHAMPION OF COURAGE

Just when we thought Sarah had overcome enough in her incredible career, the unthinkable happened. In August 2022, Dame Sarah Storey was involved in a crash during a race in Quebec that could have ended her career as a cyclist. She broke a few ribs and even punctured her lung, paving the way for a long recovery process. She was ruled out of the 2022 Worlds as she was laid up at home barely able to walk up her own stairs. On top of the damage to her lung from the crash, she contracted Covid-19, tonsillitis, and a bad chest infection, all within the span of a few months (Harle, 2023).

"I was shocked to discover my lung was as damaged as it was," she told *Sportsbeat* (Harle, 2023). "It has been quite a long recovery, and I didn't think I appreciated just how badly injured it was."

The preparation for the World Championships in 2022 was one of the most difficult and physically demanding times of Sarah's career. The accident left her emotionally shattered. It struck just when she was on the brink of fulfilling what she had poured her heart and soul into. This catastrophe hurled her into a labyrinth of psychological trials—each a formidable adversary to her physical suffering. But Sarah said she still plans to race in the 2024 Games in Paris. If her body is willing, she will be there. Not a single member of Team Storey has a doubt in their minds about that. In fact, her son Charlie is the number one motivator in this next venture. In a touching revelation to *Sportsbeat*, Sarah shared that her son Charlie had become her beacon of hope after Tokyo (Harle, 2023).

"I want to watch you at the Paralympics," he said. And suddenly, she felt reinvigorated. She was ready to jump back on the rollercoaster" (Harle, 2023).

Of course, Sarah couldn't be kept down for long. Not even a few broken ribs, a damaged lung, a pandemic, and a couple of bad chest colds could keep her from competing in the 2023 UCI Para-cycling World Championships. July 2023 marked Dame Sarah Storey's 17th road para-cycling title in the C5 Time Trial. For Sarah, securing her 42nd World title was worth pedaling through the pain (Parker, 2023). It wasn't nearly an accolade in her eyes. It was a resounding declaration that pain was just another mile marker on her path to greatness.

As you can see, it's not so simple being an athlete, let alone a Paralympic athlete who has had to change sports mid-career and somehow juggled being a mother of two on top of it all. There hasn't been a boring moment in her career as she's had to navigate through several barriers to get to where she's at today. She's risen through the ranks, fallen a couple of times, but she has always gotten back up stronger.

It's all about the mindset you have when you're taking on the toughest battles in your own life. When you choose to see these moments as stepping stools, not setbacks, you give yourself the opportunity to grow into the person you're meant to be. Don't let a small setback derail your whole life. Instead, make it your motivation to become better—whatever that may mean for you. Dame Sarah Storey wants to show everyone that it's not okay to let yourself get bogged down by life. Life grants you a single ticket for this ride, so don't forget to etch every day into your memory. Cherish your support systems. They will be your lifeline in a sea of relentless pressures. They will be your bulwark against the tide of life's challenges. And life will throw several hurdles at you to try and knock you down, but focus only on the stepping stones to greatness.

"Don't be afraid to reassess what your stepping stones toward the bigger target look like," Sarah says in her interview with *Performance People* (2023), "because there is more than one way to reach that destination."

CHAPTER 4

A LIFE BEYOND SPORT: LOVE, FAMILY, AND MORE

"It's a very selfish environment, sport," Sarah says in an interview
with *Daily Mail* (Johnston, 2021). "As an athlete you have to be
selfish. But being a parent is the least selfish environment because
you have to put the children first. I've had to work out how to do
it, but I know I can't be a happy athlete unless I'm a happy mum."

BALANCING ATHLETIC EXCELLENCE WITH PERSONAL JOY

People just assume that when you have children, you have to give up
certain things to make it work. Motherhood shouldn't be seen as
something that you "make work." In fact, it should be just as
memorable and wondrous for you as it is for your child. Sometimes this can
seem impossible with everything you have to juggle, but when you look at
people who've been able to do it so successfully—people like Sarah Storey—
you start to wonder if there is a way to balance the selfless life of
motherhood and your own selfish existence.

"People go back to work after having children in all sorts of different
physically demanding jobs," Sarah says in an interview with *Independent*
(Kenton, 2019), "so why not sport? You just have to perfect that balancing
act."

Motherhood isn't about giving up your own life, it's about creating a new
one around your child. Sarah Storey was able to restructure her career
around her kids so that she could still do what she loved while raising two
healthy children. Barney has been a key element in being able to uphold an
athletes schedule and still make sure their kids have everything they could
possibly need and more. But being a female athlete is somewhat different.
You can't be fully removed like most athletes are when they're competing
and away from home.

Sarah was eight months pregnant when she went to receive the medal that
would elevate her to damehood. Prince Charles presented the award and
Sarah recalls chatting with him about babies, as he was very excited for the
coming of his grandson in just a few short weeks. This was a great moment
to celebrate mothers as athletes and prove to other moms that you truly can
do it all. The press around that day was also centered around her baby

bump. In the pictures, they are both smiling ear to ear. First, because of the incredible honor. But also because Prince Charles cracked a joke, asking her not to give birth that day. Now, she gets to show those pictures to Louisa, who points and says, "That was me in your tummy at Buckingham Palace!" (Gallacher, 2021).

"It was a time where you have to sort of pinch yourself because there were so many opportunities and I did all of them, you know, pregnant," Sarah says in the *Stripped Back Sport* podcast (Gallacher, 2021). "I was still riding my bike and training. It just really was that perfect year."

There was an element of timing required for Sarah to make things work with wanting to have children and continue riding the athletic high she was on after the 2012 Games in London. In fact, she set herself a deadline after London, and if they couldn't get pregnant by Spring 2013, then she wouldn't be able to compete in the 2014 Para-cycling World Championships. Then they'd have to wait until another cool-down period in her career. There weren't many female athletes who were moms for Sarah to look at as inspiration, so this was unknown territory. She wasn't sure if she'd ever get to come back to sport if they didn't get a move on after the 2012 Paralympic Games (Fuller, 2021).

"Fortunately, we fell pregnant straight away," says Sarah in her interview with Aimee Fuller (2021). "Louisa arrived in the summer of 2013, and I was back on the track nine months later going quicker than I had done in London. It was crazy."

She has also come to terms with the idea that even if she didn't return to competing in sports, she'd already accomplished more than she could have ever dreamed of. This realization eased much of her mental and physical stress. Sarah didn't demand too much of her body, because childbirth already forces you to give so much. Louisa was also born by a Cesarean section, so coming back to sports was second to focusing on healing her body. She enjoyed the time it gave her to be with Louisa without having to worry about anything sport-related during the first few months (Cartell, 2013).

"My training has been different because I have been pregnant and now breastfeeding since I raced in London," she says in an interview with the International Paralympic Committee (Cartell, 2013). "The balancing act between feeds and training has been a challenge, but I love the fact that we are flexible and I just train when Louisa lets me."

By "different," Sarah means that her whole team shifted their focus after she became pregnant. They understood her needs. They carefully watched over her rigorous training to ensure she wasn't overworking her body. Everything boiled down to making sure she was okay rather than making sure she was the best she could be. There was always room for breaks so that Sarah could breastfeed on a normal schedule. With Charlie, she almost had to hang up the helmet for a while because he was a bigger baby. It took her a lot longer to get back into racing shape, and when she did, it was harder to maintain her training schedule. She tries to place very little emphasis on body composition ever since her scare with an eating disorder at a young age, but it's still important in the world of cycling. She gained a lot of muscle while she was pregnant with Charlie since he was so much bigger and she was still climbing the hill behind their house on the bike 13 weeks in. With her adapted handlebars to fit the baby bump, she happily pedaled around town up until going into labor (Fuller, 2021).

While Sarah was preparing for the 2020 Games in Tokyo, her kids were getting ready for school to start back up. She spent the whole week leading up to the event measuring her kids' feet at home, ordering shoes from her room in Tokyo, and sewing name tapes onto their school clothes. She even wishes she could do more as she calls home from different events to chat with the kids before bed (Johnston, 2021).

"They've put me on FaceTime and set the phone in the corner of Louisa's room so I could watch them play," she says in an interview with *Daily Mail* (Johnston, 2021).

Mostly, the children travel with her—giving them the same kind of exposure to outside cultures that Sarah valued so much from her own childhood—but she can't always pull them from school like she'd want to. It's always better when they do come with. Charlie's tiny toolkit which he uses to "fix mum's bike" is practically the glue that holds the Storey team together. Louisa enjoys pouring and measuring all of her mum's drinks. They just love to be involved, and Sarah loves to teach her children all about the world of sport. Nothing beats those warm hugs from the kids after a tough race.

"Disability" is not a word they use in the Storey household. Her children have never seen anything different, or missing, from her left arm. She'll laugh as she tells you that her kids call it her "little paw," asking her how it got that way and if "they can have one." She wants her children to grow up with the understanding that anything is possible with hard work and dedication. That's why it's been so important to Sarah that she brings her children along for the journey. She's raised them around Para-athletes to demonstrate acceptance of *difference*, not *disability* (Johnston, 2021). No one can tell you your limits, because limits are meant to be pushed.

Cherishing Relationships: Navigating Family Life Amidst a Demanding Career

A lot of the time, you don't get to make the decision for yourself whether or not you remain at the elite level after childbirth. Oftentimes, you lose the support of coaches, trainers, and even sponsors. Sometimes, athletes even receive backlash from their fans for their pregnancies. For example, Allyson Felix, one of the most decorated female athletes in track and field, experienced a lot of backlash from both her fans and her sponsor, Nike, which ultimately caused her to leave Nike and create her own brand. She has since spoken out on various platforms advocating for protections for maternity. She negotiated with Nike for these protections for several years before she finally gave up and left Nike (Felix, 2019).

"The one point I wasn't willing to budge around was maternity," says Allyson Felix in her Op-ed with *The New York Times* (2019), "and not because I'm planning to have another child, but just because it's the right thing to do. If not for myself, then for people coming after me."

All these limitations and strict requirements on reentering the competitive field can not only take away from mothering, but it also could put a woman's body at serious risk. You don't know what your child's birth is going to look like, and there aren't many ways to prepare for the complications that follow. Allyson Felix went in for a regular check-up at 32 weeks and gave birth to her daughter prematurely. She didn't truly get to come home until a month later. While she was worried about her daughter in NICU, she was also getting pressured from her sponsors to find gym time to be ready to run competitively in six months. To Allyson, it felt like she was "in an impossible situation" (Felix, 2019). With no way to make things work professionally, sometimes women may wonder why they'd even bother trying to adjust their family life around sports.

"As an athlete, you have a very selfish kind of existence, but suddenly you're in charge of a small person—a small life—and it's a completely sort of existence as an athlete-mom," Sarah says in an interview with *Driving Force* (Rosa, 2021, 00:43:17). "I really thrived on being able to dip into my sporting career and be an athlete those few hours a day that I was, but then to come back and have that normality of being a mom—playing on the playground and taking [them] for a walk."

The more and more women like Sarah Storey show people that being able to fulfill both roles at the same time *is* possible, the more female athletes we see being able to make strides in the sports community with their children by their side. Allyson Felix became very vocal about being a mother and an athlete after the hardships she experienced during her pregnancy. Sarah, too, makes it a point to talk about her children every opportunity she gets. Only recently have there been adjustments made in regards to topics like "Motherhood and Family Planning Elements" in sporting contracts with certain associations such as the WNBA. These plans include childcare, paid maternity leave, and even two-bedroom apartments for players and their children in some cases. However, this is only a very small percentage of athletes, and more noise needs to be made around the topic of family planning in the professional league of sports (Wray, 2021).

"There's a little mum's club. We all just quietly cheer each other on, exchange messages when someone's done well," Sarah says in an interview with *The Guardian* (Steinberg, 2016). "People say it's no different for mums than for dads, but I think it is. If a little one wakes at night the first thing they shout for is mum. So dads can go and sleep on the other side of the house—and I know cyclists who have until their kids have left school—because they don't want to be woken in the night and have their sleep disrupted. But you're never off duty as a woman."

It wouldn't be possible without her support group—her bowstrings. Remember, you can never have too many support systems, and it's good to keep a few to back you up in a pinch. Barney is a stay at home dad and both of their families are on call at any moment. Sarah's always appreciated the sort-of "family feel" around her career. It gives her something to look forward to at the races, and it gives her something to work harder for in the long run. The emotional support is something that never goes under appreciated. Every member of the Storey team, from Barney to her own parents, even down to her coaches and trainers, has been reliable and has lifted her up in some way. Her coach knew exactly what she needed during the balancing act of breastfeeding and competing at the Paralympics from his own experience at home. Sarah never had to compromise her family life for her professional career or vice versa (Rosa, 2021). Her parents have attended nearly all of her big races. If they weren't able to make it in person, they'd be smiling from behind their mobile devices watching the livestream. Her dad still holds onto every single one of her medals. Sarah's brother jokes and says it's because she's not "responsible enough to be able to have them because [she] didn't have a 'proper' job" (Johnston, 2021).

Barney deserves a medal for being able to not just take care of the children on his own from time to time, but also advise Sarah from afar, giving her valuable advice from his own experience as a Paralympic cyclist. As Sarah continues to try and better herself as a cyclist, she's able to look at one of her greatest supporters and get his advice whenever she pleases. Maybe she wants to test out some altitude training, or she wants to cut down on her time before a major competition. Barney goes straight to the books and looks for different methods and techniques that will help Sarah achieve what she wants to that week (Rosa, 2021).

Their kids are just as athletic and involved as they are, even at such a young age. Louisa is interested in becoming an Olympic swimmer, and Charlie is already quite talented on a bike. However, it's important to Sarah that these choices are made on their own without any push from her or Barney. Their schedule is filled to the top with ballet practice, bike rides, swim lessons, and more. Sarah shares just a snippet of her and Barney's schedule with Georgie and Ben Ainslie on their podcast *Performance People*, and it's incredible to think of what she's been able to achieve on top of being a rockstar mom.

"Charlie goes on a bike ride while Louisa is doing ballet on a Saturday. We tag team the acro dance on Fridays. And then in the summer months, when it's a little bit easier, I'll probably set my turbo trainer up outside by the swimming pool and do my training [alongside the kids]," she says (Performance People, 2023, 22:08).

Their day is planned out from the moment it starts, and it all centers around Louisa and Charlie. Sure, Sarah tries to be selfish at times and focus on her own career, but as she said before, it's a little bit different for female athletes. You don't just get time off from mom duty. It follows you around like, well, a toddler. But those moment's bring Sarah so much joy, especially when she gets the chance to be back in the pool training alongside her children. While she's off riding on her own, either at home or during training sessions, Barney is filling the shared family calendar planning out who is going to take which kid where and how will it fit into Sarah's schedule as an athlete. Sarah smiles down with pride at her phone as the notifications flood in each week (Performance People, 2023). It's a team effort.

ADVOCACY FOR INCLUSIVITY

Aside from being very involved at home, Sarah is also very involved in her community. As Greater Manchester's Active Travel Commissioner, Dame Sarah Storey has not just made improvements, but she's led transformative changes in the transport system. She's reimagined the city's transportation networks to ensure that they are inclusive and safe for everyone. That means cyclists, pedestrians, and drivers alike. In doing so, she's also opened up new avenues for people, especially women and para-athletes, to engage in active lifestyles free from fear. It's also important to her that she create a space for other female athletes to climb through the ranks as she did. It's a big issue, not being represented as much in your sport as your male competitors, but it's an even bigger issue of opportunity. Women aren't given as many chances to progress in their sport.

Sarah's commitment to advancing women in her sport extends beyond just advocacy. By creating a safe space for women to excel in the world of cycling, she's actively shaped this dream into a reality. In 2013, alongside her steadfast ally—Barney—she transformed her advocacy into actionable change by launching an exclusively female racing team. This created a haven for women athletes who had been long sidelined by the system. Now known as the Storey Racing Team since its official name change in 2017, this band of female athletes has become a beacon of empowerment under Sarah's guiding hand.

Composed of a diverse range of female cyclists aged 16 all the way up to their forties, the team's only prerequisite is a shared spirit of determination and a fervor to embrace their best selves—an attribute Sarah passionately pushes onto her teammates. This initiative reflects her unyielding drive to nurture a community where aspiring athletes can thrive and reach their full potential.

If that wasn't enough commitment to the advancement of female cyclists, Sarah's visionary approach led her to collaborate with the Skoda DSI Cycling Academy in 2018 to give young female athletes a chance to talk to "the right people at the right point in their career." Her involvement reflects her belief in the transformative impact of mentorship, a belief rooted in her own journey.

She developed a one-year program with the Skoda DSI Cycling Academy for women ages 18 to 24 to come and learn from her and a few other cycling professionals so that they could benefit from the same mentorship that propelled her career forward. Sarah was asked to be a mentor with the Skoda DSI Cycling Academy because of her experience as a coach and because of her history as an advocate for female athletes. In her year-long program, three or four young, female athletes can come and train under her watchful eye. Some of them even graduate to join the Storey Racing Team. Sarah's mentorship transcends mere athletic training. She prepares these young women for the multifaceted challenges that often sideline female athletes, including essential media training, which many overlook, but it is actually quite crucial for your career longevity (Spender & Cole, 2022). It's a great place for female athletes to learn that you don't have to drop out of your sporting career after high school; there are other options out there if you just keep looking.

"Having the opportunity to provide a platform for women and provide those women with a voice and the confidence to speak out and say 'this is what we need—this is what we deserve' has been one of the key parts of the Skoda investment in women's cycling and in cycling as a whole," says Sarah Storey in a video for Skoda (2022, 0:01:02).

Each year, three women are selected to join the team and they remain on for however long they choose to. Those who aren't selected still get a great deal of valuable feedback from Sarah herself. As the team grows each year, Sarah takes them to different racing events to expose them to new techniques and ideas that will help them in the long run as athletes. She encourages her team to ask questions so that she can provide the best guidance for their individual careers as possible (Spender & Cole, 2022).

By facilitating interactions between young female athletes and influential figures in the field, Sarah creates a platform for them to seize opportunities at pivotal points in their careers. This partnership resonates deeply with her as it aids athletes who might not have ascended to senior ranks swiftly, but possess untapped potential to excel at the highest echelons (Spender & Cole, 2022).

This concerted effort to bolster the journey of rising stars exemplifies Sarah's resolve to catalyze change from within her sport, a testament to her enduring commitment to propelling women forward.

"There's been a significant gap in the female pathway compared to the male pathway, which has a very established under-23 circuit of races across Europe—probably across the world," Sarah says in the *Cyclist Magazine* podcast (Spender & Cole, 2022). "So we wanted to try and provide the drive to generate gender equality in cycling and opportunity for women in the under-23 category to be able to develop."

Your average person may just draw the line there and say "I've done enough, time to focus on me." But not Dame Sarah Storey. She is focused not just on representation for women in the world of sport, but also for para-athletes. Remember, not a single one of her World Championship events have ever been televised. Coverage is so important for creating opportunities, especially for para-athletes. There are millions of girls just like Sarah who may have never even heard of the Paralympics outside of a few minutes of screen time during the Olympics. These people don't know that there are several events every single year that you can compete in against people who look like you. There's nothing for these athletes to strive for.

Media representation doesn't merely showcase possibilities. It sculpts societal narratives which build up and tear down stereotypes around ability and gender. It's a power that is often wielded irresponsibly, subsequently marginalizing female and disabled athletes (*Gender Equality in Sports Media*, n.d.). Of course, there are women's divisions and separate events that athletes with disabilities can compete in, but do you think they get as much screen time as the male, able-bodied athletes do? The answer is absolutely not.

Just as Sarah has pointed out, representation spikes around the Olympics and Paralympics. For those two weeks, you'll see more articles about female athletes and Paralympians than you will for the next four years. Outside of major events, statistics show that while 40% of all athletes are women, only about 4% of all sports media coverage is about women. And of that percentage, only a small amount of it is dedicated to their practice or achievements. Most of the female coverage for sports focuses on them as women first and foremost, not athletes. Their skills are minimized into conversations about appearance, family life, age, and they're even objectified and demeaned on live television. The other 96% of sports coverage goes to male athletes who are praised for being "powerful," "dominating," or "independent." There are so many gender-biased words and phrases used in sports media that have become problematic and need to be stopped. It's time we start opening ourselves up to what proper female athlete representation can do for the world of sports. A great way to open the doors for more discussion on female athletes is to hand the microphone over to the ladies. Female sports broadcasters would be a great way to introduce equal commentary on both fields (*Gender Equality in Sports Media*, n.d.).

"Girls need a greater number of positive role models that reach out to them on the right level," Sarah says on her website, *TeamStoreySport* (*Family Affair: Running a Women's Cycling Team*, 2017). "There are celebrated female athletes in the spotlight but for many young girls they can't identify with them and don't feel confident to aspire to be like them. By engaging and promoting women's sport at all levels we are going to have a greater impact on this age old problem of sport not being something for girls to do. It's not necessarily about creating Olympic Champions, but about providing girls with a healthy lifestyle through sport and activity."

Sarah's not just worried about the disparity between male and female athletes. She's also concerned with the lack of media representation for disabled athletes. The president of the International Paralympic Committee (IPC), Andrew Parsons, has also shifted his focus on media representation in recent years, as it can help "change attitudes, break down barriers of inequality, and create more opportunities for persons with disabilities" (Pearson & Misener, 2021). He's absolutely right. More representation would break down barriers between able-bodied and para-athletics, and it would provide people with more opportunities to reach out and advance their career as an athlete.

Representation for para-athletes is almost nonexistent outside of the Paralympics. The harmful stereotypes run rampant, even during this short stint of coverage. One of the most common stereotypes that are portrayed is the "supercrip" narrative. This frames the athlete as someone who needs to "overcome" in order to achieve greatness. Paralympians are celebrated not because of their sport, or their athletic ability, but instead because of their ability to "overcome" their disability. There is also a certain comparative narrative where Paralympians are compared to their able-bodied counterparts. The media tries to justify their success by means of the able-bodied athletes instead of focusing on their own ability to achieve (Pearson & Misener, 2021).

"I always tell riders that success is not a destination, but the journey you go through in striving to improve your personal best," Sarah says on the Team Storey website (*Family Affair: Running a Women's Cycling Team*, 2017). "Enjoying the journey—however frustrating it might be to miss out on certain opportunities because you can't afford to get there—is all part of the process. And even as a successful athlete with a multitude of medals, I still have to work hard to pay for the opportunities I want to take. Hopefully, we can all enjoy the journey together within Storey Racing, always striving to create more opportunity."

Breaking Barriers: Striving for Equal Opportunities in Sports

Breaking barriers in sports begins with equal media coverage for Paralympic athletes and women alike. This is crucial for generating excitement around these leagues and fostering new talent. It's about time we hung up these oversaturated, able-bodied male leagues. With more exposure comes more excitement. With more excitement comes more drive and determination. Without someone to look up to, or a realistic goal to set for yourself, you'll aimlessly float through life looking for purpose. Sarah is deeply committed to fixing this. She believes that filling the gaps between media coverage for para-athletes and female athletes will help make some noise around the sport and bring in new talent.

"We often talk about making riders who are resilient, but how we do that is really key," says Sarah in a promotional video for Skoda (2022, 0:00:09). "… the mechanism to generating that resilience comes from support, advice, the right environment, and also being helped and coached to make good decisions in those toughest of situations."

There aren't nearly as many events for women as there are men in the world of cycling, and Sarah is on a mission to change that. She takes her team to every event they'd qualify for to give them the necessary exposure and practice that they need in order to perform at their highest ability. There was no DSI Cycling Academy around the time Sarah was growing up, but she's thankful they're around now to help out those other athletes who may not have had the same opportunities to join sport growing up as she did (ŠKoda UK, 2022).

"Without equal opportunities at the youth and junior level," says Sarah in her video for Skoda (2022, 00:01:18), "we won't see the equality that we need at the elite and professional level."

What if she never stumbled upon that television program when she was 12 years old? Sarah constantly reminds people how hard it was to find equal opportunities for her to compete at a young age. It's hard not to lose hope of ever getting the media coverage that she deserves when not a single one of the World Championship events that she's competed in has been televised. But Sarah isn't giving up on a hope for equal representation and media coverage just yet.

The Tour de France Femmes is an all-female cycling race that mirrors the traditional Tour de France. Just like the male's race, this is a multi-day stage race that gives women a chance to showcase their strength and skill as cyclists. The Tour organizers stopped these races in 1989 because of the economic cost of running an event that had limited media coverage and little to no sponsorships (Welch, 2022). Since then, there's been an effort to bring back this symbol of equality in cycling. There have been a few equivalent events over the past few years, but in 2022, the Tour organizers declared that they were going to put on an official Tour for women. Sarah sees the return of the Tour de France Femmes as a monumental "first step" in achieving equality in cycling. Female riders now have something else to aspire to and motivate them during training (Hooper, 2022).

With the return of the Tour de France Femmes comes an influx of viewers with all eyes on the women's peloton. It also gives female cyclists one more thing to look forward to between the Olympics and Paralympics. There won't be any room for discussion of the male athletes when the events are separate and receive equal amounts of coverage from the media. It's just a matter of getting that equal amount of coverage. If we don't continue to cover these huge events in female cycling, then all of this effort will have been for nothing. Without the fans and without the coverage, everything just falls flat. Imagine trying to watch a baseball game or a football game where the stands are completely empty. You can practically hear the athletes panting over the eerie silence. This is no place to exude excitement and passion. Without the fans, you can't make it work, so there needs to be adequate media coverage to draw in that attention. People may not even realize how thrilling it can be to watch a race like the ones Sarah competes in because nobody ever sees them.

It's not a one-woman job either. Fighting for this representation is going to be a tough battle for all para-athletes and female athletes alike. It's a matter of standing together and making changes where you can. Sarah and Barney saw the opportunity to develop their own racing team for female cyclists in 2013. This was just one way of opening up the gates for other athletes down the line. Much more needs to be done to pave the way for the next generation of female riders.

A Voice for Change: A More Inclusive Sporting Landscape

You might say Sarah's plate is overflowing, but that's exactly how she likes it. As the Active Travel Commissioner for South Yorkshire, and now for Greater Manchester, Sarah wears many hats, and she wears them well. In

2019, Dame Sarah Storey was appointed Active Travel Commissioner for South Yorkshire. By May of 2022, she moved to be the Active Travel Commissioner of the Greater Manchester area (*Non-executive Board Member: DfT Dame Sarah Storey*, n.d.). She works alongside Great Manchester Transport Commissioner, Vernon Everett, to deliver a London-style public transport system to replace the current Bee Network. On November 1st of 2022, Sarah released her first report for the Mayor at an event in Wigan. Her report, "Refreshing Greater Manchester's Active Travel Mission" is meant to provide three fundamental principles to work with in the future; it details five core aspects that need to be prioritized. In the final section, it makes a few recommendations that the Greater Manchester area could adopt in order to satisfy this push for a more London-style public transport system (*Greater Manchester Active Travel Commissioner*, n.d.).

"New infrastructure alone will not solve the problem of road crime or ensure road safety," she says in her Active Travel Mission (Storey, 2022). "The feeling of being unsafe is the overarching reason many people cite when asked about the barriers they face to walking, wheeling or cycling."

The "Active Travel" part of her title refers to any form of personal means of mobility. This can be cycling, a wheelchair, a skateboard, and just walking in general. Any human-powered movement to reach a destination is included under this umbrella term. She works with stakeholders to find more safe and convenient ways for people to travel around the Greater Manchester area. With at least 92 kilometers of routes already adopted into the Bee Network, a big chunk of her job is to educate the community on the benefits of active travel. Walking, cycling, wheeling, and more are all great things to do for your health, and finding ways for more people to take part is a key aspect of Sarah's plan. She also asks people to consider the greenhouse gas emissions that are released when you choose to take your car to work every day when you work right around the corner. Studies showed that over 500 million journeys taken in the Greater Manchester area are less than three miles, and over 80% of these journeys could easily be walked, wheeled, or cycled. If we all chose to take our bikes, we could save over 160,000 tons of greenhouse gas emissions, Sarah emphasizes in her report (Storey, 2022).

"Behavior change is about more than just mode choice," says Sarah in her report, *Refreshing Greater Manchester's Active Travel Mission*, "it is also about how everyone values each others' choices" (Storey, 2022).

Sarah insists that this "hierarchy of road users must be reflected across the entirety of the Bee Network," which would mark a significant step toward making our streets safer and more accessible for everyone. Of course, Sarah is pushing for accessibility when it comes to these new additions to the plan. She wants the latest infrastructure to be universally accessible for wheelchairs and walkers alike. She'd also like to see a rise in public access bikes so that people are encouraged to be more active. Part of being able to do this is partaking in road danger reduction. She wants to hear not just from the stakeholders she works with, but from the public (Storey, 2022).

One of the biggest concerns is what's called "school streets." Sarah has been a part of a campaign as Active Travel Commissioner to make school streets more safe for children, parents, and teachers to get to and from school safely by walking or wheeling. This cuts back on dangerous emissions, but it also provides a safe road that no motorized vehicles can enter without a permit. This safe road can now be used by kids and parents alike without having to worry about a horrific accident (Oldham Council, 2023). Each one will look a bit different, but they will provide a new standard for how to behave on the road to promote safety for pedestrians and cyclists.

Walking is the biggest transportation we all use, and also the most under-discussed. Sarah wants to introduce over 800 crosswalks and 800 kilometers of extra walkway for pedestrians. She wanted to meet those standards as quickly as possible. Over the next few years, we're seeing these small changes take place. Sidewalks are getting wider, school streets are more prevalent, and the conversation around public transport is buzzing. Also, one in five people in the UK have some form of disability that could potentially keep them from using the traditional cycles. These roadways need to be made wider to accommodate for the lay-down bikes or the adapted wheelchairs (Laker & Boulting, 2022). As we witness these small changes, Sarah's relentless drive reminds us that the journey toward equality and inclusion is a marathon, not a sprint. And in that marathon, every step counts.

A LASTING LEGACY BEYOND THE PODIUM

To the average person, it might look like there's too much on Sarah's plate, but that's exactly how she likes it. Sarah set herself up to begin public speaking once she graduated university, not just to make a little money on the side, but to inspire those around her to give everything they've got to improve themselves (Spender & Cole, 2022).

"While it means you do work two jobs in many ways—in my case like seven —it gives you that opportunity to develop kind of yourself as an individual," Sarah says in an interview with *Cyclist Magazine* podcast (Spender and Cole, 2022). "…and [it] gives you ownership of what you're doing."

As a coach, mentor, and Paralympic athlete, financial concerns are secondary for Sarah. While their team, the Storey Racing Team, achieved financial stability in 2017, a large part of her work with female athletes remains on a volunteer basis (Performance People, 2023). Balancing finances with her broader mission has been an ongoing challenge. It's been difficult to find the right ways to provide for her family. Public speaking has definitely been a great source of supplemental income, but she's always looking for something more.

Creating the Storey Racing Team was not motivated by financial gain. Established on a shoestring budget, they sifted through numerous sponsors to offer female athletes a gateway to elite racing. Given the gender-based disparities in sponsorship returns, sustaining the team financially is challenging (CreativeMorning Sheffield, 2020). However, for the Storey team, the mission eclipses the financial hurdles. They are determined to create equal opportunities, no matter the cost. They knew that if they didn't try, then change would never happen.

"It's a bit of a cliché, but the only failure is not getting on the start line in the first place," Sarah says in an interview with *Mirror* (Hooper, 2022). "These riders will be able to talk about the importance of all that for the future generations because they're going through it themselves. Whether they reach the heady heights of a professional contract or not, they've seen the people within the bubble coming together so nicely and they've witnessed that triumph over adversity."

Cycling hasn't always been taken seriously by people, especially when you consider the government-protected aspect of active travel. As we mentioned before, active travel isn't just cycling, it's also walking and other forms of wheeling (like wheelchairs, skateboards, or other types of bikes). When Dame Sarah Storey was asked to be Active Travel Commissioner, her first goal was to make sure that active travel was taken seriously. Her role was to pull focus together and pull the four parts of the region together—Barnsley, Doncaster, Rotherham, and Sheffield—to create a network and a long-term strategy for reaching their goal. This doesn't just mean you'll be able to safely get to and from the store. This benefit will extend to children, the elderly, and anyone trying to get around without a car—no matter the destination (CreativeMornings Sheffield, 2020).

Under her leadership, Greater Manchester adopted four central pledges for active travel: community involvement, inclusive cycling access, safe infrastructure, and universal design. She's keenly aware of the current design flaws, such as the oversized bikes and obstructive infrastructure that under accessibility for disabled individuals. She wanted to make sure that the infrastructure being built could actually be accessed by those they intend to reach. Some of the handicapable bikes that are available are too big to fit onto the sidewalks available now. There are also a number of barriers in place that keep people from being able to access certain things like crosswalks and non-motorized-vehicles lanes. Some of these barriers include tactile paving and actual poles that are supposed to keep motorized vehicles out—but all they really do is prevent those with wheelchairs from coming in (CreativeMornings Sheffield, 2020).

When Sarah wants something, she puts her whole soul into achieving that goal. If she isn't working on improving herself, she is focused on improving the world around her. Her relentless pursuit of excellence isn't confined to sport. Sarah is a feminist and an activist. Her endeavors span beyond the athletic world, aiming to improve conditions for para-athletes and female athletes alike. If her actions can pave the way for future generations, count her all the way in.

CHAPTER 5

UNVEILING THE LIFE PHILOSOPHY: WHAT DOES SUCCESS REALLY MEAN?

"One of the things that really helps Para-athletes is when they're treated equally to all athletes," says Dame Sarah Storey (Rosa, 2021). "If they have the same opportunities, the same access to opportunities, then that inclusivity helps them to thrive."

THE POWER OF BELIEF: UNLEASHING POTENTIAL THROUGH SELF-BELIEF AND DETERMINATION

For Sarah, cycling isn't just about competing. You can be a cyclist your whole life and never race once. It can be a source of pleasure and happiness without the need to compete. However, her drive for success transformed this pastime into a fulfilling career.

"For anyone in their middle years or later years, there's always a sport to discover, and I think that's one of the beauties about sport," Sarah says in an interview with *County Linx Radio* (Ayers, 2015). "It doesn't have to be for competition. It can be for fun or for leisure. Ultimately, I'll be a cyclist for my whole life now."

Yet, when she was pulled out of the water and chose to hit the track, she was determined to rewrite history. There was a lot of doubt around whether or not she'd be able to make that switch so late in her career, but that was just another reason for her to keep pushing harder. In no time at all, she was climbing through the ranks as if she'd been a cyclist her whole life. Watching her cross the finish line in 2020 in first place, officially becoming Britain's most decorated Paralympian of all time, was like watching a superhero save the world. It was awe-inspiring, and it was proof that you can truly do anything that you put your mind to. She plans to bring that same drive for success to the 2024 Games in Paris, knowing that she has three titles to defend. During the time between Games, Sarah has to train for UCI World Championship events—and a few other supplemental races—to ensure she stays on track and maximizes her potential. This kind of meticulous planning —and a lot of help from her husband Barney—is what keeps her career afloat. She uses her experiences to help coach the women at the DSI Cycling Academy so that they, too, can have a clear vision of their future in cycling and have a plan to get there (Roberts, 2022). A woman with so many hats, and she's still so humble. When she's asked what drives this incredible determination and potential, she always says the same thing:

"I've not grown tired of trying to find the best version of myself," Sarah says in a lecture for *CreativeMornings Sheffield* (2020).

Beyond what she's been able to achieve for herself, she's been an inspiration to her community, and even her team. Sarah's goal has been to pave the way for other young, female athletes to take the stage, not steal the spotlight for herself. When she attempted to beat the UCI Hour Record on the track—a grueling test where a cyclist aims to cover the maximum possible distance on a track within one hour—she wasn't doing it for herself. This record is considered one of the toughest and most prestigious in the world of cycling. It requires an extraordinary blend of stamina, speed, and strategy. Sarah thought beyond herself that day. She was thinking about all the people watching and how she could prove that all it takes is a bit of determination and a lot of hard work. She didn't break the Hour Record that day, but she did set a new T5 Paralympic Record, as well as a British Record. Sarah rode 45.502 kilometers in just one hour. It was incredible watching her climb back up on that bike after the hour-long event—with her ice vest on and sweat dripping down her face—just so that she could take a lap around the velodrome and thank everyone who came to cheer her on. A lot of the previous riders who had attempted this record said that they'd never try it again, let alone hop back on the bike not even five minutes later just to do a victory lap (UCI, 2015b). Her confident smile said it all. It didn't matter how ridiculous she may have felt with the ice vest on, practically dry-heaving, trying to keep her balance after such a treacherous event. All that mattered was that she set a goal, and she put her all into achieving that goal.

At 39 years old, she became a World Record holder on top of already having the most Paralympic gold medals in Britain. As we discussed in Chapter Three, Sarah isn't slowing down any time soon. Now, at age 45 with several different jobs, two kids, and a very limited race schedule, she's gone on to win her 36th gold medal for the UCI Para-cycling Road World Championships. She made an incredible recovery from her injury in 2022, and despite having not competed the year before, she dominated the course (*Storey Takes 17th World Championship Title…*, 2023). How does she continue to do it all? Where does all of this incredible strength and persistence come from?

Harnessing Self-Confidence: How Believing in Oneself Fuels Achievement

I've watched several interviews of Dame Sarah Storey, and one thing that consistently stands out is her confidence as it glows from her. She's so at ease no matter who she's talking to. She doesn't blush when people start boasting about her career. Instead, she holds her head up a little more and she smiles. You can tell that it's just second nature for her. She does the work and she earns the expected outcome. The only instances that really seem to faze her are when she doesn't win gold. But even then, she uses these moments to motivate herself to push herself harder and train more efficiently for the next event.

"No one can hold your hand while you cross the finish line," Sarah says in an interview with *Cyclist Magazine Podcast* (Spender & Cole, 2022). "You have to do that for yourself."

When Dame Sarah Storey was initially invited to try and break the Hour Record by the president of UCI, Bryan Cookson, it was because they wanted to see if a woman could, in fact, set a new World Record. Of course, she leaped at the opportunity to prove herself once more. She pushed herself so hard that she could barely walk over to the chair they'd set aside for interviews. She tells them that it was "definitely the hardest hour of [her] life." And yet, she still hopped back on the bike for a quick victory lap, because nothing can keep Dame Sarah Storey down, not even her own exhaustion (UCI, 2015a).

Sarah is a strict believer in the do-it-yourself mindset. She's not one to carry around good luck charms (aside from her loving family-fan club), and she relies a lot on the scientific aspect of her abilities. In an interview with *Guardian News*, Sarah talks about how the bike is just a tool, and if you understand how to use the right tools and materials that are available, you can be successful. You don't have to "sleep with your bike in your bed" as she said with a laugh. It's about researching the latest technologies and harnessing your own abilities using the resources that are available to you.

Do you think that Sarah enjoys jumping in the environment chamber, or throwing on an oxygen mask, just to get some altitude training in? No, but it's a powerful training tool that ultimately makes her a better athlete, so of course she's going to take advantage of those things (Guardian News, 2016).

It's all about mindset and structure. It's not just about physical preparedness; it's equally about mental resilience. You're practicing not just for your body's sake, but for your mind's sake. If you can't think properly during an event, then everything else is going to fall apart slowly. Whether the stadium is packed out full of supporters, or it's so empty you can hear your own echo, you should be prepared to give it your all no matter what. Part of that preparation is maintaining the right mindset for the challenge. That requires a focused mindset capable of blocking out distractions, whether they come from teammates, rivals, or even coaches. Thinking correctly under pressure is difficult, so Sarah urges other athletes to take everything one step at a time. Prepare for the race ahead, not the races to come after. And yes, emotions do run high even for professional athletes. Sarah stresses the importance of acknowledging our human limitations. We can't control every aspect of the event, or who shows up to support or criticize us. You can't control the outcome of the event, you can't control who comes to support you—or even who comes to try and tear you down. All you can control is how prepared you are to deal with those pressures when they arise.

"The more structured and organized you are, the more likely you are to succeed," Sarah says (Guardian News, 2016).

Mind Over Matter: Strategies for Building Unwavering Confidence

Mindset is also about being able to block out the unimportant stuff. People will try to get in your head to bring you down with them. You can't let the fact that someone doesn't believe in you keep you from trying in the first place. As a competitive athlete, there are always people praying for Sarah's downfall. Whether it was those bullies from grade school, the sponsors who dropped her, or her competitors she demolished on the track, Sarah didn't allow such distractions divert her focus from victory.

"The emotion is there, that's what drove you to consider this breakaway in the first place—being opportunistic—but it all has to be calculated at the same time...." Sarah says in an interview with *Guardian News* (2016). "You can't allow [their emotions] to penetrate your thoughts. The minute you come out and off that bubble of focus, that can be when you get chased down."

Given the lack of focus on mental strength in sports, Sarah seizes every opportunity to teach other athletes about the power of mental toughness. It's far more than just half the battle. Mental preparation for your sport will help you develop a "formula to follow" as Sarah calls it. You may not know exactly how that particular race will play out, but at least you know what you need to do in order to be successful. You'll have a "principle of performance" and a mindset that prepares you for any scenario (Le Col, 2022). Mental preparation doesn't just start a few days, or a few weeks, before an event. Mental preparation needs to be a part of your regular training routine. You should be in the right mindset to train because those practices are just as important as the actual event. Especially if you're giving it your all in practice the way that you will on the road or on the track.

Of course, you should be able to hop on your bike and enjoy a good ride without worrying about preparing yourself mentally for the next challenge. But if you want to break it down even further, mentally preparing yourself to be calm in certain situations is just as important. It's a skill to be able to turn it on, and it's an even more complicated skill to be able to turn it off (Le Col, 2022). You want your brain to be ready for the task at hand. Sometimes that task is winning gold at the next Paralympics. But other times, Sarah is mentally preparing herself to be an involved parent and an inspiration to the next generation of riders.

"It's very 'that's the time to be serious and focus on the job at hand' and 'that's the time to party.' And, obviously, I used to be a swimmer, so I was very good at partying," she says with a chuckle in her interview with *Guardian News* (2016).

One way that Sarah prepares both physically *and* mentally is by using the environment chamber. We've mentioned this so-called "environment chamber" a few times, but what is that exactly? In essence, Dame Sarah

Storey trains in the environmental chamber at Manchester Metropolitan University to simulate the specific climatic conditions of various locations, such as northern Italy, to better prepare her body for events like the Para-cycling World Championships road race. It's a small room that has certain heaters and humidifiers so that the staff can monitor the conditions in the room and change them to match other environments around the world. The chamber also provides hypoxic training—which is when the amount of oxygen is altered to replicate the conditions at a higher altitude (Manchester Metropolitan University, 2018). It takes a lot of physical strength to do this type of training, but it takes even more mental toughness to do it as often as Sarah does.

"It's something that my competitors don't do, or aren't able to do," she says while talking to Manchester Metropolitan about the environment chambers (2018). "It's a quite tough type of training. I really enjoy it, even though I come out looking like I've had a shower."

Sarah would rather prepare herself mentally and physically for a challenge than rely on routine or superstition. There's no song she plays during warm-ups or a headband she wears under the helmet. It all comes down to how well she prepared her mind and body. Visualizing each stage of the competition in her head is crucial to her preparation. She checks off the steps one at a time until she's at the finish line, never allowing herself to become too overwhelmed (Le Col, 2022). A clear mindset eliminates the need for relying on luck or superstitions. You're the only one there at the start, and you'll be the only one at the finish line—not your 20-year-old teddy bear that grams gave you, or the lucky pair of socks on your feet.

"For me, I find that having to rely on something else doesn't work," Sarah says in an interview with *Le Col* on mental preparation (2022). "I prefer to soak up the atmosphere and just focus on the stepping stones I've set out for myself."

SETTING THE BAR HIGH: GOAL-SETTING AND CONTINUOUS GROWTH

When Sarah competes, she makes it look effortless. The way that she glides across the track is mesmerizing, and when she's on the road, she pushes through with so much elegance and determination that you can't help but stare in awe. Such talent and grace doesn't just happen. It takes several hours of hard work every single day. It takes intense training sessions, hill climbing, heat training, altitude tests, and so much more to be fully prepared for a multi-event sport like cycling. During the Paralympic Games, Dame Sarah Storey competes in various events, both on the track and the road, over the course of nine days. It takes months to prepare for these nine days, so she likes to keep in mind her top-five tips to keep her head above water (Voxwomen, 2017).

First, she recommends that you plan for these events as early as you can and push yourself to train under the conditions in which you will compete. Whether you're competing in the 5,000 meter race or the 500, you should make sure and do something specific to train you for each of those individual events. Don't expect to be prepared for the 500 meter race when you've only ever competed in the 5,000 meter race. Your overconfidence could be your downfall in that event. People will be training for months for their events, so you should be equally as prepared for each one (Voxwomen, 2017).

"I came here early to prepare for the course," Sarah tells *British Cycling* after the 2023 UCI Para-cycling World Championships (*Storey Takes 17th World Championship Title...,* 2023). "I wanted to make sure that I didn't leave anything out there for chance. I wanted to know every nook and cranny of this circuit and I really felt that preparation paid off. I knew what to expect, where all the bumps were and where all the rough surface was. I'm so pleased that I came here early."

Her second tip is to structure your training week according to your specific events. You should split up your time evenly so that you're distributing energy to each of those different sources. Your training sessions on each day should complement one another. You don't want to confuse or overwhelm your body too much by doing conflicting training exercises. For example, you could do sprints on a Monday and Tuesday, engage in threshold practice on Wednesday, take a short break Thursday, then spend the weekend focusing on your road events (Voxwomen, 2017).

You should also be filling your body with the right kind of fuel for the day ahead. You'll need enough energy to keep yourself going, so you don't want to get bogged down by a bunch of greasy fast food and sugary drinks. Make sure you also plan your recovery period after the events. According to Sarah, you'll use less energy on the track, but for road events, make sure that you get plenty of protein in your body to keep you running for longer. Make sure that you've considered the length of the event, and try to fuel your body enough to make it until it's over. Next, approach your preparation one day at a time. You don't need to prepare yourself for the races to come after this. Prepare for the race at hand and give your body the appropriate time to recover after bringing home that victory (Voxwomen, 2017). I'm not suggesting you lounge on the couch eating chips, but Sarah likes to celebrate her victories with her family before diving back into race-mode.

"It means you're looking at everything in isolation," Sarah says in an interview with *Voxwomen Cycling* (2017). "Once you've got one race out of the way, then you can focus mentally and physically on the next one."

Preparation is crucial. Keeping the four tips above in mind will ensure that your preparation effectively guides you. Her final tip is to let the preparation guide your performance. I once knew a coach who would harp on this idea of "muscle memory." Before competitions, we would run through our roles over and over again until it was just instinct. You didn't have to think about where to place your body because it was already there.

She often brings these ideologies to her events as a motivational speaker, as they don't just apply to athletes. Dame Sarah Storey was invited to give the Keynote speech in 2020 at the National Sporting Heritage Conference. In just eighteen short minutes, she covered a wide range of topics from her own inspirational backstory to advice on how to keep your mind and body active (Sporting Heritage, 2022). She'll jump at any opportunity to speak to the public and inspire future generations. When it comes to motivation and public speaking, Dame Sarah Storey's face is everywhere. While writing this biography, I found countless speeches, interviews, and articles about her inspiring journey. It's inspiring in itself to see her speak at so many different events in so many different roles. Whether she's wearing her cycling helmet, her swimmer's cap, the Active Travel Commissioner hat, or her activist cap, she's prepared to spread her message of strength and determination to the world.

"If you look at the opportunities that are there in your life, it is absolutely fascinating—those decisions that you make, and the impact that it has on your entire life," Sarah says in her 2020 Keynote Presentation for Sporting Heritage (2022).

Dreaming Big: The Art of Setting Ambitious Goals and Aspirations

Numerous opportunities have changed the trajectory of Sarah's life in mere seconds. When Sarah attempted the Hour Record in 2015, she had no idea she'd go in and break three other records instead. Despite falling short of the overall record by just 500 meters, she brought home the C5 Paralympic World Record, a British record, and the Master's World Record. In just one hour, she covered an astounding 45,502 kilometers on the track. She knew it was going to be one of the hardest things she'd have to do in her career, but it was an opportunity for growth, so there was no way she was going to squander it (Voxwomen, 2015). If you don't try, then you'll never have the opportunity to succeed. Sarah could have given up once she started to lose the advance she had on that Hour Record, but instead, she used the roar of the crowd to pump herself back up, and she finished strong with impeccable speed. There were no doubts running through her mind during what she would later recall as the "longest hour of her life."

"I wonder if women haven't attempted the Hour record much because our events are shorter than the men's," Storey suggests in an interview with *The Guardian* in 2015 (McRae, 2015). "There's an element of doubt in our minds when thinking about a whole hour. Men are more used to it because their time-trials and stage races are longer. In the national road race last year the men did twice the length. That's why there is more doubt for women."

Just imagine, had she not gotten a glance of the Paralympics and its athletes back in 1984, she might never have become the person she is today. An inspiration to young women around the world. In the Keynote Presentation for Sporting Heritage in 2020, Sarah talks about how her "ambition to be a professional athlete" came to her when she was watching those 1984 Games. At just six years old, her eyes were glued to the screen watching people who had similar disabilities do the stuff she wanted to be doing. There was a 15 year old swimmer on the Olympic team named Sarah Hardcastle, and Sarah said to herself "I need to be just like her." She was completely enthralled by the Games, and how the athletes prepared themselves not just physically for the event, but mentally, too. She was curious about what happened around the pool, on the edges of the tumble mat, and the process that the teams went through as they set up for their designated match. "I just wanted to experience it for myself," she says in her Keynote Presentation (Sporting Heritage, 2022).

Watching these athletes react to a win was so exciting, it made Sarah's little heart practically pump out of her chest. Their faces said it all as they crossed the finish line, landed a perfect gymnastics routine, or won their respective game. Sarah wanted to feel this level of elation herself one day. She was also motivated by the way these athletes celebrated their victories. Sarah always knew that she wanted to compete for her country in some way, but watching the way the other athletes stood on the podium and cried their heart out as their national anthem played awoke something inside Sarah. Seeing the way that these athletes reacted to their national anthem added another element of ambition to Sarah's goals. She didn't want to just throw a ball around the yard with her family anymore; she wanted to compete for her nation at the elite level (Sporting Heritage, 2022).

The presence of Olympic or Paralympic athletes in "the mixed zone"—the interview area following the events—was equally inspiring for young Sarah Storey. They would be interviewed by the press from all around the world, and "the things that they said to the press about how good it felt to be the Olympic champion made me want to experience it for myself," she says (Sporting Heritage, 2022). Sarah's mother would come in during the Games from time to time and ask her how Sarah Hardcastle was holding up. Sarah Storey looked at her mother and said:

"In eight years time, I'll be nearly fifteen and there will be a Game somewhere in the world…" she says, "and you know what, Mom? I want to be there. I want to be there for those games in 1992 and I want to win a gold medal. I want to feel what it feels like to stand on top of the rostrum and hear the national anthem play" (Sporting Heritage, 2022).

Her mom chuckled, handed her some tea, and said "sure, that's really lovely, darling" (Sporting Heritage, 2022). Little did they know that Sarah would be in attendance at the 1992 Games in Barcelona, prepared to take home the gold. They never really sat down as a family and decided that it was time for her to start competing at the elite level. The memory of watching those Games in 1984 stuck with her, fueling her motivation every step of the way during training. It stuck with her as she wrote hundreds of letters to the lady in charge of the North West Disability Swim Squad, and it was with her when she was finally invited to compete in the very last qualifying event that would propel her into the 1992 Paralympic Games. She wanted nothing more than to wear the British Olympic swimwear and stand upon that rostrum with pride.

"My dream of being at the Games the following year, the door was rapidly closing," Sarah says in her Keynote Presentation for *Sporting Heritage* (2022), "but suddenly, there was a door open, and I was absolutely delighted to head to this regional gala."

As we discussed in Chapter Three, Sarah was invited to a training boot camp after the regional gala. This is where she would soar through the ranks and catch the attention of the British Paralympic Swim Team. Her goals had finally reached fruition. All her efforts were not in vain, because she didn't give up, not even as the door was closing right in her face. Since the 1992 Games, Sarah hasn't slowed down. Her motivations stick with her as she goes through life ready to make an impact where she can. Her ambitious goals stretch beyond the track or the pool.

When Sarah gave the Welcome Address speech for the Schools' Climate Education in South Yorkshire (SCESY) in 2021, she talked about her incredible ambition to provide children with a safer space to walk and cycle to school and her plan's effects on the environment. Her role as Active Travel Commissioner allows her to contribute to her country as well as the planet as a whole. One of the most pressing concerns are gas emissions. Sarah is motivated by her goal to cut down on these harmful gasses and open up a network where people can get more active by just taking a light jog to the park or taking a slow stroll to work every now and again. There's a "huge amount of work" that needs to be done in order to change the habits of those around the UK. A lot of the problem comes with lack of accessibility and inclusion, not just for the disabled cyclists who may have a clunkier setup than most, but also for the parents who are riding "double or triple buggies" with their kids in tow (Schools' Climate Education South Yorkshire, 2021). If the roads made for these individuals aren't accessible, then what purpose do they serve?

"We need [these standards] to be enabled not encouraged," she says when asked about her plans as Active Travel Commissioner (CreativeMornings Sheffield, 2020), "because if you encourage people to use something that's not safe, then they're not going to use it because they don't feel safe. So you enable people by building that infrastructure to the right standard."

With such ambitious goals, how does Sarah Storey stay motivated through it all? Well, it's about finding what she's passionate about, and using that to try and change the world. We should be working to include those who are marginalized, especially when it comes to something as common and necessary as Active Travel. Getting from one building to another shouldn't be a battle for the guy in a wheelchair or the lady trying to push a buggy with three kids in it. There should be ample space for everyone to get around in a way that is good for our environment. Why would you need to take your car when work and school are just around the corner? If your answer is convenience, then Sarah asks that you reexamine your options for a more planet-friendly alternative.

"It makes sense to me that we want people to feel happier, and more connected to the place they live, work, and play, then they will take pride in protecting it and trying to improve it for those around them," Sarah says in her Welcome Address for SCESY 2021 (Schools' Climate Education South Yorkshire, 2021). "Similarly, the importance of accessibility is not always grasped, yet, around one in five people across the UK are estimated to be living with a disability or a long-term health condition that affects the way they are able to get around."

Staying Focused: Strategies for Maintaining Motivation Throughout the Journey

Did you know that the 1984 Paralympic Games took place in Los Angeles, completely separated from the nondisabled athletes who competed at the Olympics in New York? No? Well, neither did Sarah at six years old. But as she got older, she personally witnessed this unequal media coverage. These "disjointed Games" serve as a catalyst for Sarah's goal to unite these events and solve the disparity in coverage for disabled athletes (Sporting Heritage, 2022). As we know, a big aspect of motivation in Sarah's life is bringing about more representation for female athletes and para-athletes alike. The higher Sarah's success reaches, the more young, female athletes she can reach. As her audience grows, so does the amount of people that she impacts with her inspiring determination.

Yet, not a single one of Sarah's UCI World Championship races have been televised, and the only viewers sticking around for these incredible events are those patient enough to deal with a spotty livestream link (Fuller, 2021). A part of the problem is funding. There is a lot less money to be made covering para-athletic events instead of more traditional, able-bodied sport. This is a huge motivator for the Storey Racing Team. They race to prove—not just to their sponsors, but everyone—that there is an audience for Para Sports.

"If you can't see it you can't be it," Sarah says, "so anyone who has sort of a mild impairment as I have thinks that there's nothing out there for them" (Fuller, 2021).

And for all the girls out there who think that sport is just for boys, she wants them to understand that "everyone is welcome" and that sport is "cool for boys *and* girls," if girls are going to get more representation—and financial backing—in the future. Sarah is a bright beacon of hope for both the para-athletes of the world and the female athletes who may have wanted to drop out sooner had they not seen other women excel as she has. And Sarah knows there is a long road ahead to encourage young women's participation in sports and counteract the trend of women leaving sports more quickly than men (Fuller, 2021).

Getting nominated for BBC's Sports Personality of the Year Award in 2021 was a huge step in that direction. A para-athlete has never been nominated for this award, so to even be in the running was an honor (Fuller, 2021). It showed Sarah that she's still working hard to achieve new things in her career. She's not just sitting at home waiting for the next Paralympic Games. Instead, she's out there making a difference as one of the greatest motivational sport's personalities of all time. Because, no matter if the world is watching, or if it's just her husband and kids logged into the spotty livestream link or her latest event, Sarah is going to give it her all. She may not always return with the gold, but she's going to hop on that bike and prove to the world that both female athletes and para-athletes are capable of greatness regardless of the outcome. With both sides of that coin on her side, she's an inspiration to millions of girls and boys around the world.

Unfortunately, as a cyclist, you need to be aware that you won't always be at the "top" of your game. Sarah warns other cyclists that training at the elite level is done in cycles. You won't always be at your so-called "peak" because these periods are short and should be taken advantage of. Part of motivating your own journey is taking it one step at a time. By this, I mean you have to time your peak out for the event you're training for. You won't always be at the top end of your physiology, but if you know what you're preparing for, you can be ready when the time comes. According to Sarah, your peak comes around about three or four times a year. When she was trying to navigate through training during a global pandemic, things were extremely uncertain, and dates for events kept changing. This made it nearly impossible to schedule the training cycles in an efficient manner. But like every challenge Sarah's been faced with in her long career as an athlete, she mustered up all her strength and she drew upon her incredible resilience to make it work (CreativeMornings Sheffield, 2020).

Even when the Coronavirus pandemic shook the world and sent everyone home packing, Sarah continued honing her athletic prowess independently. When the Women's Tour of Britain was announced to be a virtual race, Sarah took her personal laptop and set up a stationary bike in the garage. She hung up a dusty sheet behind her to cover the stuff she didn't want people to see, and she raced from home. It was a unique experience, but it didn't have anything on actually being there in the race with the wind whipping your cheeks and the sun shining down on your back. Sarah often refers to her garage as the "pain cave," because, even without the fancy equipment—like the environment chamber or the velodrome—she was sweating it out in her garage at the same level of intensity and drive as she was before the pandemic. While she's unable to achieve the 80% humidity level, that's normal inside the environment chamber, she is able to put a few heaters in the garage and throw on her hypoxic mask to mimic those conditions

(CreativeMornings Sheffield, 2020). You're the creator of your own destiny. Sarah shows us that you can't let anything stand between you and your dreams. She started as a young girl who wanted nothing more than to compete and win for her country. Now, she's inspiring millions of other young girls around the world to take an active role in their own lives. Put yourself out there, and don't hold back once you've been handed the spotlight.

"It's the unknown that can be the most unsettling, but that's the physiological and mental challenge," Sarah says (McRae, 2015).

CHAPTER 6

KEY LIFE LESSONS: STORIES THAT INSPIRED THE LEGEND

"I always tell riders that success is not a destination but the journey you go through in striving to improve your personal best," explained Sarah on the Team Storey Sport website (*Family Affair: Running a Women's Cycling Team*, 2017). "We have an ethos which we hashtag for social media as #BestVersionOfYou. This defines our approach and provides riders with a focus for their journey. We are entirely process driven, ensuring everyone focuses on the nuts and bolts of a performance rather than the outcome goal."

RESILIENCE IN THE FACE OF ADVERSITY: TRANSFORMING OBSTACLES INTO OPPORTUNITIES

It took Sarah a while to realize the strength in being resilient. When she was growing up, she was bullied relentlessly for her passion and her drive. This kept her from "fitting in" in everyone else's eyes. But she learned over time how to harness this thing called resilience. You see, according to the Merriam-Webster dictionary, resilience is a noun that refers not just to "the capability of a strained body to recover its size and shape after deformation," but also the "ability to recover from or adjust easily to misfortune or change" (Merriam-Webster, n.d.).

According to Sarah, once you've experienced enough, and you've developed this sort of "thick skin," then you can "see off anyone or anything." That is a powerful tool, maybe even more so than being physically strong (Sporting Edge, 2014). We talked a lot about mental toughness in the last few chapters, but I can't emphasize enough how important it is to embrace your challenges and hardships as a part of you. These are pivotal moments where you can learn the most about yourself. Do you think that Sarah could have ever accomplished the things she has if she had let the bullying she received in school push her out of the pool for good? Would she have become the most decorated female Paralympian of all time if she hadn't made the switch to cycling after those persistent ear infections in 2005? Probably not. Sarah has used her resilience to bounce back from so many barriers on her way to success.

According to a report published in the *Journal of Sports Sciences*, psychosocial resilience is essential in sport because they have to withstand a number of pressures. Mustafa Sarkar and David Fletcher examined the psychological resilience in Olympic champions to better understand how these athletes utilize and optimize "a range of psychological qualities to withstand the pressures that they experience." Somehow, these athletes don't just hold up under pressure—they thrive. They looked at things like proactivity and motivation and determined that athletes have a way of keeping their eyes on the prize despite any challenges that step in the way. Olympic athletes have several motivators in their lives including social recognition, passion for their sport, achieving personal goals, and proving their worth. They "actively chose to reform in challenging sport environments" because they value the strain it puts on them, and the fact that it forces them to grow and adapt. This appears to have an impact on their mental strength and ability to ignore negative stressors. They also found various sources of confidence were prevalent amongst the world's greatest athletes including multifaceted preparation, experience, self-awareness, visualization, and a great team backing them (Sarkar & Fletcher, 2014). Sarah has always tried to harness each of these unique characteristics at every stage of her career. Her dedication and focus has been unmatched. Focus was yet another thing that Sarkar and Fletcher found was an important aspect of resilience among elite-level athletes. They even talk about how focusing your cognitive energy on the "task at hand" can have positive effects on performance. Sprinters who use race plans have been able to run faster than those who use a baseline, or control (2014). Being able to focus on one task at a time has given Sarah a chance to excel at everything she does. Her mental toughness has gotten her through difficult times, and each time, she chooses to simply focus on the task at hand.

Athletes deal with all sorts of stressors on top of what they handle at home. This can be injuries, a dip in their performance level, organizational conflicts, pressures to perform, and so many more. That's why resilience is so essential. It protects us from the potential negative effects of these stressors. It's not just a mindset, but a collection of coping strategies that guide you during a rough time. It can enhance your self-esteem and motivate you to do better (Lapp & Davidson, 2020). In Dame Sarah Storey's case, she's always known exactly who she is. She's identified her personal motivations, her goals, and she's always been willing to try new things. These are great ways to improve your confidence and recover from hardships (Lapp & Davidson, 2020).

One such motivator is the tube of Jelly Babies she keeps in her pocket during her training sessions. A lot of athletes that have been considered the pinnacle of health and fitness actually have their own little guilty pleasure snacks to keep them moving. A lot of preparation goes into every ride, but Sarah refuses to forget her Jelly Babies before leaving the house. Sure, the two large water bottles with pre-workout are great, and the cereal bars she recommends are fantastic for you, but everyone needs a little sugar boost now and again.

"Once the bottles are made up, and the food has been sorted, the final thing that I do is make sure that I have enough Jelly Babies," Sarah says in a vlog on her YouTube channel, *Storey Channel*, (Storey Channel, 2023c). "These are absolutely vital—I find—during the final hour of a ride when you need just a little bit of a sugar boost to get you home."

From Challenges to Champions: Turning Adversity into a Source of Strength

People often view setbacks as failures. Not Sarah. Instead of letting this sense of discouragement and loss of motivation ruin her ambition, she used this as an excuse to better herself. Researchers say that you should evaluate your setbacks constructively. Instead of getting down on yourself, ask yourself what you've learned from this experience and how you plan on tackling these setbacks in the future (Lapp & Davidson, 2020). Dame Sarah Storey is no stranger to adversity. She's battled through bullying, chronic fatigue syndrome, countless ear infections, and a horrendous crash which nearly rendered her unable to compete. Any one of these things could have caused her to hang up the swimmer's cap or the helmet, but Sarah turned her adversities into a source of strength time and time again. Do you think Sarah truly wanted to compete with the British Swim Team in the 2000 Paralympics after her coach told her she was getting "too old" at the pre-Paralympic trial in 1999? What about when she competed in the 2004 Paralympics in Athens after learning that her mother was diagnosed with cancer? Dame Sarah Storey has been building up this "thick skin" for years, and there isn't a thing that could keep her down for too long. While it may seem impossible in the moment, overcoming your hardships will allow you to grow and come out stronger on the other side. We've seen this in Sarah's life many times.

Sarah was training in London just 10 days before the widespread lockdown in 2019. COVID-19 took the world by storm, and it impacted everyone, especially our beloved athletes. At first, everything was unknown. Sarah's trainers weren't sure what protocols they could take in order to get her back into a normal training routine, and nobody was sure how to go about getting tested in order to ensure the virus hadn't spread through the gym already. Once the dust had settled a little, Sarah was told she should train on her bike out on the road just once a day. They didn't want her practicing in an enclosed space, and Sarah was determined to get back on the bike to keep up her fitness level. As we know, Sarah got around not being able to go to the gym by transforming her garage into a "pain cave" during the course of quarantine (CreativeMornings Sheffield, 2020). This was just one way for Sarah to turn adversity into strength. Maybe her other competitors could have set up their garage similar to Sarah's and kept pace in the 2020 Paralympic Games, but they just didn't harness that same drive as Sarah did.

Slowly, more and more races began to open up, and Sarah was happy to be able to stretch her muscles beyond the confines of the "pain cave." Of course, track races took a bit longer to open back up, but she was smart and proactive enough to have pushed to learn both techniques early on. Getting through quarantine was just another thing to test and strengthen her resilience. One more thing to demonstrate Dame Sarah Storey's ability to overcome anything she puts her mind to. Some people were pushed out of the things they loved most during such an uncertain time, but not Sarah. Her entire team stood behind her and banded together to help find a way to keep Sarah at peak performance when the races would eventually return. Her husband, her kids, and her racing team all worked collaboratively to create a schedule that worked for everyone. And let's just say, her kids definitely got more say when she was stuck at home.

Sarah once said that creating a winning mindset allows for enjoyment, meaning that these competitions are supposed to be just as much fun as they are intense. She says "it's supposed to be fun," and you also get to enjoy the time you get with those that you brought along—like family and friends. "Team is a word that we use in so many ways," Sarah says. It's not just the actual people out on the track or the road competing. Instead, your team can also be those who are working behind the scenes that "make things happen." Sarah's team is built around loyalty and dependability. You want the people working with you to truly understand you—and not just in an athletic sense, but in a personal sense. You want them to understand your needs and your desires so that you can all work toward the same goals. Sarah didn't have a steady "team," or even a singular coach for that matter, until she became a cyclist. Now, she works with the same people day-to-day, and it only raises her confidence more and more as they grow more comfortable with one another. While a lot of her training is done on her own, her team still acts as an advisory board who can help advise her as a person and an athlete so that she can excel (Champions Speakers, 2023).

"A winning mindset is an incredibly individual thing, and I think that the way that you start is to think about where you want your end product to be —what your end ambitions might be—and have a variety," Sarah says (Champions Speakers, 2023). "If you meet one of them, then knowing where you are going to go after that is just as important."

It all goes back to this idea of following the "stepping stones" and not trying to get too ahead of yourself or else you'll fall in the water. You're creating your own pathway to success, so use your ambition to reach each goal one step at a time. Don't overwhelm yourself by thinking two goals ahead. Allow your expectations to be flexible, and you'll be much more satisfied with the results. There might be a new way to reach that next stepping stone that you hadn't even considered before. Make one change at a time because you want to be able to edit yourself if something didn't work before. Sometimes you have to pause and take a rest in order to grow. It isn't always about running full speed toward your end goals.

And when things don't go to plan, it's time to get back up and try something new. Sarah once said "the race plan didn't exactly execute according to plan," after racing in the rain at the 2020 Games in Tokyo. Instead of letting the outside conditions impact her performance, she relied on her hours of training at home in the rain to guide her actions (BeanymanNews, 2021). She used mental toughness and muscle memory to push through and come out on top.

"It was a very different race than the one I anticipated," Sarah says (BeanymanNews, 2021), "and in the end, it was actually the descents that made the difference more than the climb."

Grit and Grace: How Resilience Shapes Dame Sarah's Approach to Life

Let's talk a little about an award we haven't discussed yet. In December of 2020, Dame Sarah Storey was awarded the Bill McGowran Trophy by the Sports Journalists' Association (SJA). This award is the first award to recognize excellence in disability sport. It was first introduced in 1963. They recognize and highlight the accomplishments of a para-athlete every year, and in 2020, it was Sarah's time in the spotlight (Sports Journalists' Association, 2020).

Typically, this award ceremony would take place at an exquisite gala in London, but because of the difficulties with the COVID-19 pandemic, the 2020 SJA awards were held virtually. Yet, Sarah was still dressed to the nines behind her laptop screen in an elegant sequin dress. She was excited to share her experience as a young 14 year old girl in her first Paralympic Games in Barcelona. She boasted about how the choices she made as a young girl created a path to greatness that she's been riding along ever since (Sports Journalists' Association, 2020).

"I didn't really know what to expect, that's for sure," she told Karthi Gnanasegaram with SJA (Sports Journalists' Association, 2020). "I also knew when I came home that I just wanted to be an athlete forever. So I guess I'm holding true to that statement."

THE STRENGTH OF COMMUNITY: BUILDING SUPPORT SYSTEMS FOR SUCCESS

As I said earlier on in this chapter, Sarah has been working with the same cycling team since beginning her cycling career in 2006. Her team has provided a great sort of professional and personal mentorship that has lifted her up and given her plenty of opportunities to succeed. Without this team there at her beckoning call ready to answer questions like "would this new training technology benefit my career?" or even "should I be maintaining a diet during the downtime between events?", Sarah would probably be grasping for straws trying to figure it all out on her own. Barney, her husband and first official mentor in the cycling world, has been an incredible source of information and motivation for Sarah.

"I think it's a really valuable way of working—knowing who your mentors are, who your sponsors are," Sarah says, "and when you're not in a room, is there somebody in there who can think about whether or not you would benefit from something within that space" (Champions Speakers, 2023).

Teamwork and Triumph: The Importance of Coaches, Mentors, and Collaborators

The Storey Racing Team started as a way for Sarah to get control over her own cycling program and training (Rosa, 2021). It was first and foremost a place for Sarah and Barney to finally separate from the other trainers and coaches and begin working together one on one. When Louisa was three months old, they got their first sponsor, and the Storey Racing Team was born (well, not exactly under that name quite yet, but you catch my drift). As we said before, Sarah's career has always had this sort of "family feel" around it. Both her and Barney's parents live close by, and they're always ready to jump at the call for help. And they don't just provide support for the family. Sarah's parents are often found at the gym alongside the Storey Racing Team, bringing them healthy snacks, making sure they have enough water, and providing support where they can. They bought a motor home together, and they loan it to the Storey Racing Team whenever they need to travel to a competition (*Family Affair: Running a Women's Cycling Team*, 2017).

"It's not cheap to enter and attend a UK race either," Sarah discloses on their website TeamStoreySport, "as unlike UCI events there is an entry fee per rider to pay and no accommodation or food provided as happens at UCI events. As most UK women's races start at 9 a.m., every race requires overnight accommodation and we try and provide an evening meal too as riders wouldn't be able to race very often if they also had to pay for hotel meals every time" (*Family Affair: Running a Women's Cycling Team*, 2017).

Barney says that the motor home has made life easier and even reduced the cost of travel significantly. They wish they could do more for the team, but making life easier where they can ultimately takes the pressure off of the team so they can focus on their events. Sarah's parents are always tagging along, ready to show off their Scout Group skills and cook for everyone (*Family Affair: Running a Women's Cycling Team,* 2017).

"Hopefully we can all enjoy the journey together within Storey Racing," she says, "always striving to create more opportunity."

In most cases, an athlete's perceived social support refers to their access to social support as well as their perception of whether or not their teammates, coaches, and friends would provide assistance if needed. With more social support comes "higher levels of self-confidence and lower levels of burnout" (Sarkar & Fletcher, 2014). Sarah has had a plethora of different social supports that have only made her stronger. Each time she looks out in that crowd and sees her parents, her husband, and her kids, her passion and determination is refueled, and she's able to bounce back from anything. Aimee Fuller, a fellow Olympic athlete and podcaster, asked Sarah if she thinks that motherhood has given her some sort-of inconceivable strength. Sarah chuckled in response before saying "you know, maybe!" (Fuller, 2021).

Some athletes aren't as lucky to be able to bring their support systems with them along this wondrous ride. That's okay, because social support doesn't just mean family. It can also mean your coaches, support staff, and your teammates. Having these people to lean on during stressful events can provide this almost buffering-like effect. Social support is multidimensional in nature, and it can refer to four different primary dimensions, including emotional, esteem, informational, and tangible. First, emotional support refers to the fact that others are there for comfort and security. This can help someone feel loved and cared for. Next, esteem support refers to how well someone can lift up your spirits and overall sense of self-esteem. Informational support is how much guidance or advice you can get from someone (Sarkar & Fletcher, 2014). This is often the type of support that you will receive from a coach or trainer. Finally, tangible support refers to the concrete, instrumental assistance that you get from someone. It's found that when people have these social supports in their lives, they find stressful encounters to be less stressful. In the case of athletes, they feel less pressure when they know their coaches and teammates are there to support them. Their self-confidence levels are raised, and when you have high levels of available esteem support, competitive challenges are seen as less of a threat (2014). Instead of looking at each competition as a challenge that she has to overcome, Sarah looks at it as an opportunity to share a fun and exciting experience with her family and her teammates.

We know that her old swim coach, Alastair Johnson played a huge role in her career as a swimmer, but Sarah's experience with cycling has been a little different. She began her experience as a cyclist with mainly mentors who had seen her around the gym and noticed that she had some serious potential on the bike. People like Barney would come around and encourage her to try new things, and eventually, her mentors would guide her onto the British Cycling Team. Her coach on the British Cycling Team, Dr. Gary Brinkley, was actually the coach she's had the longest. They've worked side-by-side for over 11 years, and he knows the ins and outs of her training routine as if it were his own. He was actually a triathlon gold medalist himself, so he had an incredible amount of knowledge concerning what it was going to take for Sarah to switch her "swimmers body" into a "cyclist's body" (University of Brighton, 2016).

"That knowledge and that understanding and that empathy for what I was going through was absolutely invaluable," she says (University of Brighton, 2016), "and I think that part of my sort-of speedy switch was down to the fact that Gary had that understanding."

Triumphing Together: The Power of Shared Experiences and Celebrations

Plenty of athletes would have retired by now. What keeps Sarah pushing for so long? When asked this during her presentation for CreativeMornings Sheffield, she says that she looks at her career as this incredible jigsaw puzzle. She hasn't grown tired of finding new ways to make things work, not just on the bike, but at home, too. In her day-to-day life, she takes on several roles being an athlete, a motivational speaker, a coach, and of course, Active Travel Commissioner, but so far, her favorite journey has been motherhood. It has made her lifelong journey "just a little bit different," but in the most beautiful way possible (CreativeMornings Sheffield, 2020).

When asked about how it feels to come back into training after being pregnant and having children, Sarah says (Inspired Exchange, 2017): "I always said that going into cycling as a second sport was a massive bonus, and now I feel like I'm on my third bonus."

When Louisa was born, she was immediately drawn to the pool and to the bike. She loved coming to all the different events to shout "Go Mummy!" and wave her flags. Maybe it had something to do with the way she watched her mother smile from ear to ear while competing. Or maybe Louisa was born to be an athlete just like her mother. Either way, Sarah never wants to push her children to do anything. She'd never force her kids into cycling just because it's what she loves. In fact, Sarah says she'd learn a whole new sport if it was something her kids loved (Ayers, 2015). Louisa is currently into acro dance, which is something Sarah never would have imagined trying. She had also played table tennis, net ball, cross country, and whatever else could get her heart racing.

"I'll be right behind [them] in whatever [they] choose to do," she says in an interview with *County Linx Radio* (Ayers, 2015). "If I have to become an athlete in a different sport, then so be it."

I don't doubt that for a second; we've already seen her do it once before. But, as we said before, Louisa is actually drawn to the pool the same way her mother was as a kid. Earlier in 2023, nine-year-old Louisa Storey challenged her mother, Dame Sarah Storey, to a race in the pool. In an adorable vlog for the Storey Channel on YouTube, Sarah and Louisa put on a small skit to show the competitive nature—and supportive community—in their household. They even got Charlie involved. He smiled ear to ear as he entered the scene. Louisa started the video by asking her mother to be her training partner for the aquathlon— a multi-sport event consisting of both a swimming segment and a running segment—to which Sarah responded (Storey Channel, 2023b):

"An aquathlon? I could swim, but I can't run, and I don't have any kit."

"No problem, Mummy!" says Charlie as he enters with the kit on a dinner tray.

With all of the appropriate gear on hand, Sarah had no choice but to accept Louisa's challenge in this sprint aquathlon. Sarah allows her daughter to walk her through all of the necessary steps and transitions involved in this event, and they even do a bit of stretching together before diving in. Sarah held the lead in the pool, but as soon as they hopped out and raced toward the track, Louisa was hot on her trail. Behind the camera, you can hear Charlie cheering for his big sister shouting "Go, Louisa, go!" And in no time at all, Louisa took the lead.

"Yay, Louisa! You won!" Charlie says when his big sister crosses the finish line, heaving and looking around to find mum. Sarah was found on the ground in obvious exhaustion. When Sarah admitted defeat, Louisa responded with a light-hearted "I smoked you" (Storey Channel, 2023b).

The Storey Channel on YouTube is relatively new, but it does capture a number of heartwarming moments between Sarah and her family. She and the kids enjoy making vlogs, and Barney makes a great cameraman. This channel is just another aspect that brings about that "family feel" to her career that we've talked about so much. When they aren't focused on Sarah's training, or the kids' lessons, they're out in the world showing their kids that sports are exciting, and not just for men. Louisa and Sarah went to the Netball Super League Season Opener, and you can see the obvious excitement on Louisa's face when she talks about the venue. Sarah always tries to make these experiences educational for her kids to keep them curious. Even as they dined in a private room before the event, Louisa was glued into the books about netball and the players they'd be watching that day. You could tell that Sarah was so proud to watch her daughter get excited about something that she used to play—and loved very much. Sarah took her daughter to get autographs from the star players, and she talked to her daughter about some of the incredible skills and tactics these women were using that could inspire them both (Storey Channel, 2023a). These videos are a demonstration of the passion that Sarah has for sport and the ways she's passed that down to her children. You can see firsthand just how involved Sarah is as a mother, despite also being an elite level athlete. This just isn't something you see in male athletes who are parents.

The only exception to this is our dearest Barney Storey. Sarah also loves to boast about her husband because of all the incredible work he's done not just for Sarah's career, but for their life in general. Barney Storey transferred to stay-at-home-dad duties in 2013 after retiring from the Paralympics himself (Performance People, 2023). He's been there for all of her victories as a cyclist, and even through a number of personal victories. When she first found out that she was being nominated to become a Dame, Barney was right there beside her. In fact, he grabbed the post that day and casually tossed it on the table. When an envelope with the Royal Crest on it slid out from the middle of the pile, they both shared a curious glance before leaping to grab the letter. It was pretty heavy, so she knew there had to be something important in there. When she opened the letter and read "you've been nominated for a DBE," she was actually flabbergasted (Ayers, 2015).

"What's a DBE?" she asked Barney.

"That's Dame! Commander! Oh my goodness!" he said.

For those like Sarah who are still a little unsure, remember that "Dame" is an honor granted to women after they've achieved a certain level of respect from the British Empire. It stands for Dame Commander of the Order of the British Empire. It's the female equivalent of knighthood. They had to keep it quiet for a while, but it was nice having someone who knew. Barney planned this huge dinner with their whole family on Boxing Day and decided they would share it with everyone then—even though it was two days before it would be officially announced. When everyone was sitting down around the table, Barney stood up to propose a toast (Ayers, 2015).

"Everyone needs to stand," he said, "because I'd like to propose a toast—except for the lady who's pregnant. You can remain seated, my dear."

Once everyone was standing, he raised his glass and said "Arise, Dame Sarah Storey!" Everyone in the room went absolutely ballistic. Cheers rang through the house and everyone gathered around Sarah to congratulate her (Ayers, 2015). Sharing those moments with people that you love is truly what it's all about. Sarah is so thankful to have such a loving and supporting team —and fan club for that matter—alongside her every step of the way. People always ask her how it feels to have been bestowed such a great honor.

"I still pinch myself, but ultimately [the honor] is shared with so many people because the career I've had wouldn't have been possible if it hadn't been for a huge amount of help," she says in her interview with *County Linx Radio* (Ayers, 2015). "I hope I can use the title well to help other people in the future."

HARNESSING PASSION AND PURPOSE: DISCOVERING PERSONAL GREATNESS

When Dame Sarah Storey decided to add motivational speaking to her repertoire, it was almost like a necessary next step in her career. Of course, she didn't plan on hanging the helmet up anytime soon, but there were times where she felt like she wasn't reaching enough people being stuck on the track or zipping through the road. She had a goal in mind to change the world of sports, and she couldn't just do that from the track or the pool. Interviews after the events were pretty short, and they never wanted to talk about the broader sociological aspects of sport. Sarah wanted to get out into the world and talk to as many people as she could. She wanted to raise eyebrows about representation, talk to sponsors about all-female racing squads, and find a better way for para-athletes to be represented outside of the Paralympics. As we've seen throughout her journey, Sarah has joined a few companies as a motivational speaker, and she began attending different events to talk about resilience and facing adversity with your head held high.

One such company, *Champions Speakers*, published an interview asking Sarah how she would guide businesses to align themselves with her goal to bring equality to those with disabilities. She started off by saying that businesses should do their best to replicate duties for disabled employees so that they have access to practically the same work as nondisabled employees. This is the kind of model they use at the Games. Next, the "trajectory for people should be the same," meaning you shouldn't "lower your sights" if someone has a disability. In fact, many people with disabilities have said that it only pushes them to work harder and demonstrate their ability in any context. People with disabilities are just as ambitious, just as hard working, and just as qualified to be an employee as the next able-bodied individual. Lastly, celebration of success is important because you want to be able to celebrate everyone's victories evenly. This doesn't just mean giving credit where it is due for disabled employees, but also not being demeaning by celebrating the smaller victories rather than the larger ones.

"You should celebrate everyone's success in the same way," Sarah says in her interview with *Champions Speakers* (2023), "and make sure that everybody has that opportunity to feel that their contribution was valued and that they're part of that bigger team."

Living with Purpose: Aligning Values With Actions for Lasting Fulfillment

Since becoming Active Travel Commissioner, Dame Sarah Storey has tried to close this glaringly obvious gap in access to safe active travel for disabled individuals versus nondisabled individuals. Of course, she wants everyone to participate, but she's noticed a severe problem with the way that people with disabilities are forced to get around day-to-day. Without ways to exercise and improve their physical health, Sarah worries that their mental health may be at stake (Access Sport, 2022). As Active Travel Commissioner, she has also taken on the mission of eliminating deaths and serious injuries within the city-region. Her plan, cleverly called "Vision Zero," is meant to make it "safer, healthier, and more sustainable place for pedestrians, cyclists, motorcyclists and motorists." In 2021, there were about 858 deaths as a result of motor collisions in just the Greater Manchester area alone. Vision Zero plans have already started to be implanted, such as 20 mph speed limits, safer crosswalks, and increased enforcement for speeding vehicles (Transport for Greater Manchester, 2023).

"Any death or serious injury on our roads is one too many, and these collisions are already devastating people's lives…" Sarah says in an interview with *Greater Manchester Moving* (Transport for Greater Manchester, 2023). "These incidents are neither acceptable or inevitable, and we should all be doing everything we can to prevent them."

Sarah's efforts to make the roads safer for everyone has also had a huge impact on the safety of children getting to school. The new "School Streets" are meant to ensure a safe journey for children to get around the block and to school safely from their homes. Roads are closed off, and only cars with certain certifications and licenses can come down these private roads. It gives children access to the whole road to avoid any incidents. The extra activity also allows them to be more active in the morning. This can lead to a more positive day, and a more relaxing evening. Sarah traveled to a school in

Chorlton in March 2023 to observe some of the incredible benefits of this plan (Storey, 2023c).

"It was very uplifting and demonstrated perfectly why investing in walking, wheeling and cycling has far reaching positive consequences for today, tomorrow and the bright futures of these fabulous children," Sarah says on her LinkedIn profile after the event (Storey, 2023c).

Thanks to all the effort that has already been made to make Great Manchester a safer place for active travel, they have been able to play host to stage one of the men's race at the Tour of Britain in 2023. The "entire spectrum of cycling was on display," and Sarah was even presented an "amazing rainbow bands Bee Bike" in celebration of all her success as Active Travel Commissioner, and her performance at the World Championships a month prior. She was able to talk about her plans for the new infrastructure and also demonstrate what her actions have already done for cyclists in the Greater Manchester area (Storey, 2023b).

"Inspiration to participation isn't always easy to translate," Sarah says in another LinkedIn post (Storey, 2023b), "but there's an even bigger drive across the region, and I'm looking forward to building on this momentum as we wait to find out if Manchester's bid to become European Capital of Cycling for 2024 is successful and other new participation and infrastructure plans are announced."

Participation is an essential aspect to inclusion. Like Sarah says, if you don't see people like yourself in a particular role, then you probably think that it's not possible for people like you to take that role. Lack of access for women or para-athletes to certain events has hindered athletes for too long. It's about time we open up more opportunities for these people to compete so that we can set the right example for future generations.

Unleashing Greatness Within: Embracing Individuality and Finding Identity

So what have we learned about Dame Sarah Storey so far? She's not just a prolific athlete. Sarah is a mentor, a coach, a mother, an activist, a hard worker, and just an absolute inspiration to us all. We know that she doesn't hit the road without her tube of Jelly Bellies, that her children are her greatest motivators, and that she is going to keep fighting for the rights of women and para-athletes until she physically can't anymore (Storey Channel, 2023b). Sure, she's got a million different things going on all at once, but if you tried to take away any of those aspects, I'd hate to be in the crosshairs. Whenever a new opportunity arises, you better believe that Sarah is the first to jump the gun. She's always anxious to get her hands on the latest technologies and training methods, as Sarah is willing to try anything that could potentially make her even better than before.

When you switch careers so late in the game, oftentimes, people are waiting on your downfall. With Sarah, she picked up cycling so quickly, there's no doubt that she received some backlash from her fellow competitors. But even if so, it would only motivate Sarah to push harder and edit herself so that she does better the next time. Cycling requires a lot of alone time with just you, your bike, and the road ahead. You have to be "good in your own company" as Barney Storey says (Performance People, 2023). Sarah has always been good in her own company. Her confidence and determination are key during these long hours of training on her own. Without some sort of internal compass guiding her to a better self, she wouldn't have been able to succeed as she has.

Though, she's not totally alone out there when she has the company of her racing soundtrack. Sarah has a unique soundtrack of all her favorite songs that were playing during her different events. Each song elicits a unique feeling and memory distinct to that venue or city. Coldplay's *Paradise* is one of the songs that remind her of the 2012 Paralympic Games in London (BBC Radio 6 Music, 2014). This was such a momentous Game for para-athletes because the coverage of the Paralympics that year was on par with that of the nondisabled athletes in the Olympics, so of course it's one of Sarah's fondest memories to reflect on.

"It just seemed to sort of describe what everyone was thinking," she says in an interview with BBC Radio (BBC Radio 6 Music, 2014). "This was the *paradise* of athletes. This was exactly where we wanted to be. For those of us fortunate enough to win gold medals, we were in our element, and it was just incredible—it was paradise!"

Every time that song came on the radio—for weeks to follow—Sarah would be filled with this overwhelming sense of pride and accomplishment. Her heart would thump as she sang along, and tears would threaten to fall from the corners of her eyes. It would throw her back into that moment, standing on the podium, listening to what felt like the greatest song of all time. The "heroes that those Games created" get to carry these memories, and this connection to music, with them for the rest of their lives (BBC Radio 6 Music, 2014). When Sarah is older, and Coldplay comes on the radio, she'll look back fondly on these memories she's made, and the accomplishments she's had, and will continue to have until she decides to hang up the helmet.

But that won't be any time soon. Even if she were to move beyond the world of professional sport, she would still be deeply enthralled with all things athletics because that's just who she is. She'd probably end up coaching one of her kid's sports teams or dedicating herself full time to coaching the Storey Racing team. She's made it clear that she never wants to push anything onto her children because she wants them to find their own passions. Still, Louisa has gravitated toward the pool, not because of her mother, but because she's seen the way that it impacts their life and well-being. Louisa wants to follow in her mother's footsteps because her mother's footsteps are so inspirational.

CHAPTER 7

LEGACY AND INFLUENCE: AN INSPIRATIONAL TALE

"As athletes, we do continue to strive and push forward to make sure that inclusion and diversity is always at the forefront," Sarah Storey says in an interview with *Champions Speakers* (2023). "Everyone has something to offer, and allowing the conversation to be opened up to more people is a very valuable tool for us all."

BEYOND MEDALS: INSPIRING A GENERATION TO REACH BEYOND LIMITS

The London 2012 Games have been celebrated as the catalyst for bringing harmony between the two disjointed events: the Paralympics and the Olympics. Sarah, while hoping that she would eat her words, said that while the effort was there, this was still a challenge that would need to be overcome at all the future Paralympic Games.

"We knew that the Paralympic Games had an opportunity to transform the lives of people with disabilities who are athletes," she says in an interview with *Champions Speakers* (2023), "but being able to transform that into a social environment was always going to be a challenge."

With the work that she's done as an activist and a public speaker, Sarah does believe that we're on the right track to finding that balance of representation. The conversation has been sparked, and now, all there is to do is fan the flames and hope that this idea catches. It's so important to have that equal representation, because as we know, you're more likely to imagine yourself in roles that are visible. If you're an athlete with a disability, but all you've ever known is able-bodied sports, you may give up on your dream too soon without looking outside of the traditional sports media coverage. If we were to get accurate coverage—not just during the Olympics and Paralympics, but all the time—then we'd be able to see those challenges that our disabled athletes have to go through. It would allow us to continue this discussion on resilience and change the way we think about "ability" in terms of able-bodied and non-able-bodied athletes.

The work that she's done with Skoda DSI Cycling Academy has been in efforts to try and progress women into the professional peloton. Did you know that male cyclists make wages off some of their races? Others make minimum wage no matter which race they compete in. Women find it much harder to seize lucrative racing opportunities. Oftentimes, they have to do what Sarah has done and look outside the world of sport for supplemental income. This is because there isn't what they call a "under-23 category" for women like there is for men. So, young female athletes have less opportunities to make money at the beginning of their career while men can graduate out of the junior ranks and go into the under-23 for a time (Warwick, 2021).

"Some women miss out on the transition into the senior peloton," Sarah says (Warwick, 2021). "The step out of junior ranks into senior can be really daunting. I was approached with the hope of setting up something within women's cycling."

Impact on Aspiring Athletes: Encouraging Others to Pursue Their Dreams

Along with the lack of representation, there is also a lack of access for women when it comes to elite-level and international competitions. For the most part, women haven't been able to replicate the success of their male counterparts because "the void between domestic and world-level racing is too great." There are plenty of small races to compete in year-round, but they aren't as well funded, they aren't as big of a test to your ability, and they aren't inclusive of para-athletes. Women haven't been able to enter this "tiered system" of competitive racing that men are so accustomed to. Men have at least three to four different tiers when it comes to races, and they have the ability to move through these tiers for teams and riders. This isn't the case for female riders. It's one and done for athletes like Sarah, and she wanted there to be something done about the fact that she can't compete against people at her level if all women are considered to be one-tiered racers. Women's races are shorter, celebrated less, and rarely covered by the media (*Dame Sarah Storey Keen to See...*, 2015). Women want the opportunity to prove themselves just as much as men. Sarah believes that changing the women's ranks to resemble their male counterparts will draw more motivated women in. they may even push themselves a little harder than they did before.

"We now really need to see some step changes in the events that we ride in the UK," she says (*Dame Sarah Storey Keen to See...*, 2015). "It's quite obvious that what we call the 'elite' level in the UK is still a way behind elite level in Europe and other parts of the world."

With more female cyclists being celebrated as professional athletes at the highest rank, a wave of female cyclists is bound to come. In fact, in 2013, there were a quarter of a million less women regularly cycling on the road compared to in 2020 (*Dame Sarah Storey Keen to See…*, 2015). This number just keeps rising as Sarah makes it safer for people to be on the road at all as Active Travel Commissioner.

"…those mass-participation events are absolutely superb," Sarah says when talking about her many cycling campaigns as ATC, "and now we need to see that legacy drifting up the pyramid and really challenging the girls right at the very top, because that is where our Olympic medals and Paralympic medals come from" (*Dame Sarah Storey Keen to See…*, 2015).

Since becoming Active Travel Commissioner, Dame Sarah Storey has been involved in a number of events, programs, and fundraisers trying to push for a safer, more accessible network for people to travel in. One program in particular, Wheels for All, has had a significant impact on making sport, and cycling in general, more accessible to people with disabilities. It's a nationwide group of cycling programs that have gained popularity across different social media platforms. They can be found all over, including in Wales, Scotland, Northern Ireland, and England to name a few. They want to increase the density of access to bikes for those with some form of disability (CreativeMornings Sheffield, 2020). Through help, support, and guidance, people in different local communities across the world are given a chance to cycle on a regular basis (*Welcome to Wheels for All*, n.d.).

"Our plan is that, if more people can feel enabled to actually use a bike in the first place—by the time we get this infrastructure built—it will enable people to have a bit more independence."

Sarah was a part of the Wheels for All program that took place in Hillsborough Park, and here, she's been able to help other cyclists test out the machinery, and get access to important resources, before having to make these purchases themselves. They get to see the different options available to them, and it allows them to test these bikes in an area that is traffic free. People can also get free professional help in what they should look for in a bike and get some guidance from people like Sarah before investing in the wrong materials (CreativeMornings Sheffield, 2020).

"It was brilliant to see the session unfold and the smiles it brought to the faces of everyone who'd attended," Sarah said on her LinkedIn after the event (Storey, 2023a). "I love riding the trike too!"

Oftentimes, people are stuck waiting for assistance getting from point A to point B, and in reality, these points are not that far from one another. You should be able to hop on your adapted bike and get yourself there without being dependent on a caregiver or family member almost 24/7. Sarah would rather you enjoy the wind on your face and the breeze running through your hair than sitting in a crowded area waiting for your ride (Storey, 2023d). That's why she's continuing to go out of her way to push for a more integrated active travel plan that will allow for more people to get out of their stuffy cars and onto the new, safer sidewalks and cycling lanes. She's worked with many different organizations to see this through, and she's not letting up anytime soon.

"Visiting councils that are pulling together a bigger plan and knitting together the many facets of an integrated active travel and public transport system is always a pleasure," she says on her LinkedIn profile (Storey, 2023e). "…As always I asked my usual mix of questions about things like cycle parking, disability access, non-standard cycles and enabling journey chaining with a mix of modes, and was really pleased with the discussions we had. Looking forward to seeing more school streets and more progress in the coming months."

Spreading Hope: How One Person Can Shape the Future

Beyond any personal interest in sport, Sarah urges our younger generation to remain active for the sake of their health. By increasing accessibility, she's able to bring hope back to this idea that staying in shape can be fun. You don't have to sprint to work every day to remain active, but if you had access to a city-provided electric bike, or some other unique form of travel, getting to work could be something you look forward to each morning. When asked "why is this so important to you?" Sarah says:

"Because of a lack of activity, and because we've prioritized being able to go door-to-door in a vehicle, we're actually reducing people's outlook for the future" (CreativeMornings Sheffield, 2020).

We've never had a more inactive population. For the first time in several decades, kids aren't expected to live as long as their parents or grandparents did. Prioritizing inactivity has resulted in a number of health controls across the globe. Active travel can actually play a huge role in our healthcare system when you consider the positive effects of staying active. Reducing how often a certain ailment appears within a population will ultimately reduce the cost of care for that health concern (CreativeMornings Sheffield, 2020). For example, if we can get the number of people with Type 2 Diabetes to decrease, so will the cost of treating such ailments. It will also help people maintain their health and live a longer, happier life. Exercise is a proven cure-all for those struggling with mental disorders, which is why it's important that we get these measures in place to make exercise accessible to all. It can help people better manage their conditions.

"This is a global challenge," she says, "and we have to access this globally. But, here in the Sheffield city region, we can all play our part. It's important for health, and it's important for well-being" (CreativeMornings Sheffield, 2020).

Among many other events, Sarah recently volunteered to ride with the Radnor Primary school for their regular Friday Bike Bus route. Instead of taking the bus, these kids have started a regular biking route to take to school on Fridays. They travel through a series of roads, junctions, and roundabouts to pick up kids along the route and safely migrate to school as a group (Storey, 2023d). This is exactly the kind of stuff that Sarah wants to see moving forward with her plans as Active Travel Commissioner. Initiatives like this give kids a chance to be in control over their own health. It also allows for a cleaner earth, less rambunctious kids on the last school day of the week, and it does exactly what Sarah wants to see in all kids: It keeps them active.

REDEFINING GREATNESS: LEAVING AN INDELIBLE MARK ON SPORTS AND SOCIETY

Remember how I mentioned that the Storey Racing Team didn't have the rights to that name until 2017? Well, before they were team Storey, they were actually the Pearl Izumi Sports Tours team (cyclingnewstv, 2015). This was one of the sponsor-driven names that Sarah references when she says that they had to change names so many times in the beginning because of unreliable sponsors. While it wasn't quite the name they wanted, Sarah and Barney still managed the team themselves and would continue to push for accurate representation for female athletes.

"We wanted to put together a program that would allow me to really excel as an athlete," Sarah says when people ask what drove her to create this team (cyclingnewstv, 2015). It was a place where she could try out her own ideas, test her own limits, and shake things up without having to worry about her trainers, coaches, and mentors believing that they were a waste of time.

"Once you're at the top, there's only one way to go, and that's down," Sarah says (cyclingnewstv, 2015) so we needed to make sure I could stay as one of the leading Paralympians in para-cycling."

The team has only grown since its creation in 2013 after Louisa was born. Now, they have twelve riders, and Sarah works closely with each one to ensure that they are finding the best versions of themselves to bring to the competitions. These women have learned so much about elite-level sporting, and Sarah only hopes to be able to provide more in the future when opportunities for women open up. She enjoys teaching these young women about confidence as well as handling disappointment. Sarah hopes to pass on her mantra of resilience to each one of the riders under her wings.

"It's been really fun, and I think that's the thing about sport; it has to be fun first," Sarah says in an interview with *cyclingnewstv* (2015). "Although you sort-of look at my palmaris and think 'wow that's a lot of things to do' everything has always been a great fun as well."

Transforming Definitions: How Dame Sarah Storey Reshapes the Notion of Greatness

Even during some of her most challenging times, she's kept that big, bright smile on her face. At every opportunity she has to interview and talk about her journey, she's beaming from ear to ear. After winning her 17th gold medal at the 2020 Tokyo Paralympic Games and becoming the most decorated female Paralympians Britain has ever seen, she did a live interview with Sky Sports News.

"It's definitely not sunk in; it's been the most incredible day," were her first words on camera (Sky Sports News, 2021).

At the Tokyo Games in 2020, the riders had to endure fog, hail, and sideways rain on top of the challenging factors that were already involved. Sarah takes training very seriously, so she's made sure to train in as many different conditions as possible, but you can only simulate so much. If there had been no bouts of hail leading up to the event, then there likely weren't any ways to train for how these conditions would impact the ride. But Sarah didn't let herself overthink. She took it one step at a time, and finished strong without letting the conditions affect her ride. In fact, she said she was joking around in the pit before the races saying that she "asked for these conditions" because she felt that she was prepared to take on anything (Sky Sports News, 2021).

"I actually quite enjoy racing in the rain when there's no vehicles around," Sarah says (Sky Sports News, 2021). "It's quite different, and the roads look quite different. I got all the faith in my equipment. I have great tires on my bike that I know will stick to the surface. You know, I can go around the corners in the wet just as quick as I can in the dry, so I was quite happy with the conditions."

The spray off the wheels was really the only unexpected challenge having trained alone. Sarah never faltered though, and she maintained a positive and determined mindset that pulled her to the finish line—even when she had to race with her eyes shut to keep out the rain drops. She competed in three events, always adhering to her motto of just taking it one race at a time. Sarah tried not to focus on the pressure of breaking the current record for most gold medals held for a Paralympian. Her focus was on performing to the best of her ability. She didn't even realize what was happening until she was in her third race realizing "It's mine! It's mine!" as she glanced over her shoulder every now and again (Sky Sports News, 2021).

"If I am absolutely honest, it's still taking me time to work it all out," she tells an interviewer from Rouleur (*In This Extract from the Road...*, 2022). "Normally, when you finish a race, you feel as if your legs have worked the way you wanted them to. I'd never been in a championship race before when my legs have not done what I asked them to do: a combination of the lack of road racing preparation and maybe the cold, too. So slowly it's been sinking in that perhaps my brain was the winning factor. Though I was physically in great shape, I had to use my brain even more than normal. The tactics were not straightforward."

Three decades of success, eight Paralympic Games, over forty World Titles, and still, she plans to compete in the 2024 Games in Paris to uphold her position as Britain's most successful Paralympian of all time. She tells *Sky Sports News* that she wants to plan a big bike ride with her team from Manchester down to Paris. She doesn't know if they can make her dream come true, but she still laughs and says it would be "a really cool way to arrive at the next Games." Since Charlie hasn't been to a Paralympic Game yet—well, nobody could really attend in 2020 because of complications with COVID-19–she's still got that goal in mind. She absolutely adores being able to share these experiences with her children.

"There's so much that's happened," she says in her interview with *Sky Sports News* (2021). "We've also worked so incredibly hard, and we've sort of had this big jigsaw puzzle, and there's still pieces to fit into it—it feels like."

One puzzle piece at a time is all you can really handle, but when it comes together, it creates a much larger picture. To onlookers, Sarah's life is a huge success full of nothing but wonder and excitement, but when you pull back those layers and take a look at each piece, you can see how hard she worked to get there. Nothing just fell onto Sarah's lap. She's had to go out into the world and find every opportunity for growth that was out there in order to climb those stepping stones to success. Sarah has known that she wanted to compete for her country since she was just six years old, but it still took her about 24 years to fully bring these dreams to fruition. She never gave up hope. From her first gold medal ever, in the 100-meter backstroke in 1992, to her most recent victory at the UCI Para-cycling World Championships in 2023, Sarah has been surprising people and making a difference in the world of sports for women and para-athletes alike.

In her very first event, she was up against a German swimmer who had never been beaten before. Sarah was the first person to beat her by knocking just three short seconds off of the German swimmer's world-record time (BeanymanSports3, 2016).

"I just remember how excited I was at the fact that I had actually beaten her," she says to *BeanymanSports3* (2016). "I just never stopped smiling for the rest of the week. I won another gold medal in the tourna-medley and then came home and realized that this is what I wanted to do with the rest of my life."

Breaking Norms: The Everlasting Impact of Redefined Boundaries

Dame Sarah Storey has a never ending list of championship titles, awards, honors, and medals. On top of what we've already discussed in Chapter Three, Sarah was named Deloitte's official London 2012 athlete ambassador (Deloitte UK, 2012), she was Female Paralympian of the Year in 2013 at the Cosmopolitan Woman of the Year Awards (SuperPopVIP, 2013), and she was nominated for BBC's Sports Personality of the Year in 2016 (RoryOConnorTV, 2016).

"For me, it's all just a part of the great journey towards the top of the podium," she says (Deloitte UK, 2012).

When Sarah qualified for the England team in 2010 and joined them for the Commonwealth Games in Delhi, she had no idea that this would make such a wave in the search for equal access for para-athletes. She just wanted to find more opportunities to compete at the highest level, without there needing to be a distinction between disabled and not. But regardless, it was a huge moment for para-athletes, and it should be celebrated as a huge win. There weren't just more eyes on her, there were more eyes on the entire community of para-athletes. She's always been a multi-event athlete, so there has been plenty of chances for her to show everyone what she's made of. When an interviewer from the *Huffington Post* asked if she's ever experienced any low-points in her outstanding career, she reminds us where her incredible determination comes from (Packham, 2017).

"I don't think the low points have ever resulted in me wanting to throw in the towel," she says (Packham, 2017), "rather, they reinforce my motivation to either overcome the adversity of the injury, illness or disappointment, or to prove the doubters wrong. When times get tough, it's usually the point that my husband and I get our heads together to work out a new strategy."

Sarah has shown us plenty of ways that we can succeed in our own lives. One thing that she always harps on is not doing it alone. Whether you're an athlete, a business owner, an artist, or even a fast-food chain worker, give it your all, and don't be afraid to lean on the support systems you have around you. What does it take to be a champion? It takes time, hard work, determination, and a dash of fun. Because, what else are you doing all this for?

"I choose a process-driven approach that ensures I'm searching for the best version of me," Sarah says when asked what her motivational mantra is (Packham, 2017). "My biggest motivation is to find the peak of my physical capabilities. I hope this allows me to keep adding different stimuli and trying different approaches, alongside my tried-and-tested methods to push the personal best times and performances."

A RIPPLE EFFECT OF INSPIRATION: CATALYZING CHANGE AND EMPOWERING OTHERS

When Sarah was asked to return to Leeds—the town where she went to university—and actually speak to university students, she was ecstatic to be able to speak with the young boys and girls that were in a position she found so pivotal to her own career. University was an extremely tough period in Sarah's life, and she battled a lot of demons that she wouldn't wish on anyone. That's why she finds it so important to speak to the youth about her experiences and let them know they're not alone. If she can help motivate someone to step out of a dark period in their life and try something new, then she'll be there, whether it's a student-led interview, a video conference call with a classroom of students, or even a small bike riding event in the park (Inspired Exchange, 2017).

When she arrived in Leeds, Sarah was asked to partake in the Uni-Girls-Can week at the university. It was an honor to be considered and included in something so close to her heart. It's important that everyone has a healthy, balanced lifestyle, so when Sarah had the chance to promote getting women into sport, it was an opportunity she couldn't miss. Leeds Student Television interviewed Sarah about the campaign and its perceived effects, to which Sarah responded that promoting anyone—not even just women on campus —to be more active is the goal. However, she knows that women in university are less likely to be involved in sports because they were either bullied out of it sometime in high school, or they decided that sports weren't for women to succeed in the same ways that men have.

When Sarah was in university, she already had five gold medals to her name. The discouragement that she received as a kid rolled right off her back as she raced through the ranks as an elite-level athlete. The wonder and excitement surrounding the Games is still present every time she's in attendance. She tells the student interviewers about the vending machines at the Olympic Games and how they don't require any money, so you can just grab as many Cokes as you'd like in theory. She also gushes about being able to "rub shoulders with the sort of athletes that were there" because she was able to stand tall beside some of her greatest heroes. And, they would even eventually become her greatest mentors and supporters during her own incredible rise to success (Inspired Exchange, 2017).

People always ask Sarah how she does it, but when the Leeds Student Television interviewers asked Sarah how she was able to balance being a professional athlete and a student, it was with genuine astonishment and curiosity. These kids were doing everything they could just to get up early enough that day and get ready for an interview that would take place after sitting through four-to-five boring lectures that day from an equally burned-out professor. How did Sarah keep her head during it all? Her secret was to combine what she loved with what needed to get done. She combined her studies with her passion for sport. Of course, it was still difficult, and if you recall, Sarah did end up spending a lot of her time at home away from university trying to rest her mind to prepare her for the next day.

"I was really fortunate that I had access to so many elite athletes, so when [my professor] came to do my dissertation for example I was able to study some of the best athletes in the world," she says (Inspired Exchange, 2017). "I had access to all sorts of different swimmers around the country, that I would ring up and ask if I could do testing on them."

Inspiring Action: How Dame Sarah's Story Ignites Others to Make a Difference

As the new British Cycling policy advocate, Sarah's goals have remained clear: Make a world where everyone can be active and healthy. You don't have to be a professional athlete to be a cyclist. You can hop on your bike every single day, or just once a week, and still be a cyclist if it brings you joy and keeps you active (British Cycling, 2017). Find what makes you tick, and get out there in the world and be the best at it that you can be. If you've learned anything from Sarah, it's that you don't know what's going to happen down the road, so there's no sense in worrying about what you're going to be doing a few years from now, or even what you'll be doing next week. Focus on the task at hand, and put all of your effort into it. That's how to be successful in all aspects of life.

Sarah treats every meeting, every practice, every interview, and every competition the exact same. They're all moments in which she has a chance to make a difference. So of course, she's going to shine as bright as she can so that she can grab the attention of other young boys and girls who may have shut sport out of their life a little too soon. How could you watch Sarah talk about her drive and passion for sport and not wonder if you could have loved something that much? Do you find the same joy as she has in your own career? If not, maybe you've found yourself in a position where you can actively change your outlook on life by taking the wheel. Instead of letting other people guide your existence, start taking a more active part in your life. Stand up for the things that you believe in, try new stuff that interests you, say what you mean—and say it loud—because you've only got one shot at this thing called life. Don't squander it trying to make other people happy. There will always be people who are going to look at your life and tell you that you should have gone down a different path. You might even hear this from the people that you thought were in your corner. Take a lesson out of Sarah's playbook and evaluate your support system closely. If they're not lifting you up and encouraging you to seek out your dreams in life, maybe they weren't meant to continue supporting you forever.

Challenges are not placed in your way to prevent you from moving forward. They're there to help you grow beyond the limits you already possess. Do you think it was easy for Sarah to make the switch from full-time swimmer to full-time cyclist? Sarah never imagined herself as a cyclist—even when she was racking up title after title in different sports throughout grade-school—which just goes to show the importance of keeping your options open. People often forget how strong of a swimmer Sarah was now that she's made such a groundbreaking debut in the world of cycling. Thanks to Louisa's interest in swimming, Sarah still gets to show off her skills in the pool during her daughter's training and also on their YouTube channel, *Storey Channel*.

But, as Sarah has shown us, her family is the greatest achievement of her career so far. They are the "foundations of making it all work." Without the help of her family, Sarah doesn't think she'd be able to make it all work.

"They represent a lifetime of work and commitment to something I have thoroughly enjoyed putting so much time and energy into," Sarah says (*Dame Sarah Storey Talks Reaching…*, 2021).

One of my favorite stories I found was about Louisa's first experience at the Paralympic Games in 2016. After each event that Sarah raced in, she would bike over to the part of the crowd where Barney and Louisa were sitting front row, and she would be able to kiss her daughter and show her how much she loved her. When Sarah was standing on the podium, Louisa started to cheer for her mum. The national anthem started playing, and it echoed through the stadium. Louisa seemed to think it sounded a lot like the soundtrack from her favorite movie, Frozen, so she began belting out her rendition of *Let it Go*. Sarah and Barney both say that it was so special watching her have so much fun. Having her daughter in the crowd doesn't distract her at all. In fact, it motivates her to push harder and do better than she did at the previous Games (Gordon et al., 2016).

"To make other people happy and proud is huge," she says (Gordon et al., 2016). "After London everyone thought I should retire on a high but I knew I could still go faster and today's proved that."

Empowering through Example: Encouraging Individuals to Overcome Challenges

It doesn't have to be about sports for Sarah to want to get involved. There have been several opportunities for Sarah to get involved with her community without having to show up dressed in her tracksuit with gold medals in tow. One of her most recent calls to action has been bringing an end to the "heartbreaking" period of poverty that plagues our society. There are problems all over the world with lack of access to free or affordable sanitary products. In places like Scotland, women and girls have access to free pads and tampons, and England and Wales have been pushing to be brought in that same line.

"It's heartbreaking to hear how young women and girls are unable to manage with dignity every month," Sarah says (Connor & Killelea, 2022). "When it feels like you don't have control, it can have huge effects on confidence and mental well-being."

Studies have shown that those who can't afford tampons are less likely to come to school or social events during their time of the month and that means ruining sporting events in some cases. For people like Sarah, this just can't happen. She doesn't have the option of clocking out when her time of the month is on. Even if they wanted to reduce their symptoms by exercising or remaining active, most people still wouldn't be able to without access to sanitary products. The campaign that Sarah has chosen to back has taken a number of steps to open up access to free sanitary products including reaching out to state and government buildings to get free products put into their bathrooms, they've begun working on a mobile app that can tell users where the nearest place to access free sanitary products is, and they've started marketing to a larger audience (Connor & Killelea, 2022).

As a mother of a young girl, and an activist and supporter of all women, this is something that Sarah feels very passionate about backing. Period products are essential to life. When you don't have control over your body during such an already complicated time, it can affect your confidence and well-being. There are also a number of teams that compete with white—or just light-colored—shorts, which can be anxiety inducing if you're a professional athlete and you know that your period is just around the corner (Connor & Killelea, 2022). She's also concerned with how much, or really how little, women pay attention to their ability to check themselves for cancer. Breast cancer is a huge concern for women all over the world, but in her little corner of the world, Greater Manchester has the lowest rate of breast cancer screenings in the whole country. Breast screening is offered by your gynecologist after the age of 50, and cervical cancer screenings are available after the age of 25. However, you can still check yourself for abnormalities if you educate yourself on what is considered normal for your body versus what would be cause for concern. If you're worried about something, then you can go see a doctor before it grows out of hand (Answer Cancer, 2021).

"Screening for cancer early helps us detect any problems, and to get it treated, so it really does save lives," Sarah says (Answer Cancer, 2021).

A Legacy of Empowerment: Sparking Positive Change in Communities Worldwide

When it comes down to it, there isn't an area of life that Sarah hasn't tried to perfect in some way. She's taken on sport to make a difference for people like her, she's found love which has brought her immense happiness and two beautiful children, and she's continuing to make a difference in everything she's a part of. From the podium to the road, Sarah is trying to make a safer and more accepting community for all people. Her ability to align her personal values and goals with her practical abilities has been unmatched. If she had set her sights on going to the moon, I don't doubt for a second that she would have made it happen. Her journey has just been one incredible stepping stone after another.

In order to make positive change, you have to be consistent. Sarah has had the same set of values and goals since she was just a little girl. She's wanted to make a difference for her country by whatever means necessary. She was written off by her peers, her competitors, and even potential coaches because of her disability and because of her sex. Had she let this isolation keep her from going to all these different countries, competitions, and experiences, she would never have been able to become the inspiration that she is today. There are several moments that can completely derail this roller coaster called life, and how we react to these changes is what dictates our future. Sarah has taught us that resilience is invaluable, and harnessing your inner power to make a difference is the greatest way to demonstrate that strength.

CONCLUSION

What more can I say about such an incredible inspiration to our generation, and for generations to come? Dame Sarah Storey will only continue to change the world as she progresses through her career as an athlete. Her career has always been multifaceted. It was never just about sports. It was about fitting in and helping others do the same. This long journey has not come to an end, because Sarah has yet to see an equal playing field for people like her. Being a woman, and a para-athlete, she has a unique perspective on the lack of access and coverage for female athletes and para-athletes. Sarah has done everything in her power to make sure that her personal values align with her actions.

Sarah has been a public figure since she stepped on the scene as an elite level swimmer as a young teen. She changed what people thought was possible when she switched sports mid-career and became a cyclist. And Sarah jumps at the opportunity to hop in front of a camera and share her story. If she didn't put herself out there, she wouldn't have been able to make the stand she has. All of her work as an activist has given her the opportunity to test out several roles to see where she can make the greatest impact. Once she was nominated Dame, she didn't think there was any better way to reach a greater audience. But in just six short years, she was also nominated to be Active Travel Commissioner for Greater Manchester. Stepping into this role has opened several doors for her career outside of racing. And yet, all of her work still centers around the same idea: Making a more accepting world for women and people with disabilities.

Dame Sarah Storey hasn't slowed down since the Barcelona Paralympic Games in 1992. She started at such a young age, and it seems like she's always known exactly who she wants to be. Nevermind that she was a swimmer when she started, and now, she's making new kinds of waves as a cyclist. It didn't matter what role she was playing at any certain time. She just wanted to make a difference for her country. Sarah wanted to represent her nation proudly, and she's done that with confidence every step of the way. I'm not saying that everyone should be competing at the elite level by the age of 14, but there is something to be said about that drive and determination. This kind of passion is what gets things done.

You don't have to be going into an Olympic Game to be at the top of your game. If you bring the same attitude and mindset as Dame Sarah Storey into your everyday life, I promise that you're going to get a lot more done. We talked a lot about this idea of maintaining a positive mindset and harnessing resilience, but this is something you have to actively work for. Believe in yourself and your abilities, and that confidence will help you soar above those stressors that constantly try to pull you down.

Dame Sarah Storey has overcome bullying, chronic fatigue syndrome, persistent ear infections, the birth of two children and learning to balance motherhood with her career, and even a very nasty crash in 2019 that almost led to an early retirement. It was her unwavering spirit that brought her out of these hard times—stronger than she was before for that matter. There hasn't been a challenge that Sarah felt she couldn't overcome eventually. She never had to do it on her own, though. Let's not forget about the importance of having a solid team in your corner. Sarah has had a number of supportive people in her career that have opened new doors she may have never considered before. She's had incredible coaches, mentors, teammates, and most importantly, she's had the help of her loving family. Take a look at some of the people in your life who have lifted you up in some way. Have you thanked them recently? Maybe it's time to consider the ways that other people have helped you get to where you are now.

With everything that we've learned from Sarah Storey, it would be a shame for you to continue to squander your talents. Don't let your worries and doubts keep you from putting yourself out there in the world. Always keep your eyes open for new opportunities, and keep your chin up, too. As Sarah has shown us, confidence is key to overcoming any obstacles that life throws at you. There isn't a thing under this sun that you can't accomplish if you just put your mind to it. That is why Sarah is so adamant about maintaining a positive mindset. You never know until you just try. What is something that you've always wanted to do, but you've always been too scared to give it a try? I dare you to harness your inner Sarah-Storey-strength and give it a go. You never know; this could be the thing that will change your life forever.

REFERENCES

Access Sport. (2022, July 19). *Dame Sarah Storey Talks about Access Sport's Partnership with Nuffield Health*. Video. https://www.youtube.com/watch?v=s-HpYyvtQIk

Answer Cancer. (2021, April 15). *Dame Sarah Storey Talks about Cancer Screening*. Video. https://www.youtube.com/watch?v=Srzb1qI0I6E

Ayers, A. (2015, June 2). *Dame Sarah Storey*. Www.youtube.com. Video, 0:04:56. https://www.youtube.com/watch?v=02VX7l04pzc

Barney Storey. (n.d.). TeamStoreySport. Retrieved on August 11, 2023, from https://teamstoreysport.com/barney-storey/

BBC Radio 6 Music. (2014, July 5). *Dame Sarah Storey's London 2012 Soundtrack*. Video. https://youtu.be/97fXYBAai50?si=TKfUB3Iu22rNQT-S

BeanymanNews. (2021, September 2). *Dame Sarah Storey 'very Proud' of Paralympic Success*. Video. https://www.youtube.com/watch?v=TVCKZmDzJno

BeanymanSports3. (2016, September 9). *Dame Sarah Storey On Becoming GB's Most Successful Female Paralympian*. Video. https://youtu.be/8THwnQhNZPQ?si=pSjB7u0Xs8GMjEjy

Blitz, S. (2021, January 12). *Dame Sarah Storey on Battling the Bullies, Eating Disorders and a Coach Who 'didn't Train Disabled Athletes' on Her Journey to Becoming Britain's Greatest Ever Paralympian... and the Swimmer-turned Cyclist Has Tokyo in Her Sights*. MailOnline.com. https://www.dailymail.co.uk/sport/othersports/article-9135513/Dame-Sarah-Storey-opens-life-struggles-way-Team-GBs-greatest-Paralympian.html

British Cycling. (2017, May 3). *Dame Sarah Storey Is the New British Cycling Policy Advocate*. Video. https://www.youtube.com/watch?v=Lwzdwv1WfOA

Brown, O. (2021, December 6). *Dame Sarah Story Exclusive Interview: 'Surviving School Bully Equipped Me for Challenges Ahead.'* The Telegraph. https://www.telegraph.co.uk/cycling/2021/12/06/dame-sarah-storey-exclusive-interview-surviving-school-bully/

Cartell, S. (2013, September 4). *One Year On: Sarah Storey Becomes a Mother*. Paralympic.Org. International Paralympic Committee. https://www.paralympic.org/feature/one-year-sarah-storey-becomes-mother

Champions Speakers. (2023, April 25). *Sarah Storey Speaker | How London 2012 Transformed the Lives of Disabled People | Contact Agent*. Video. https://www.youtube.com/watch?v=NHRP1NElvxs

Classification in Para Cycling. (n.d.). International Paralympic Committee. Retrieved on August 9, 2023, from https://www.paralympic.org/cycling/classification

Connor, L. & Killelea, A. (2022, November 19). *Paralympian Sarah Storey Backs Mirror's Calls to End 'heartbreaking' Period Poverty*. Mirror. https://www.mirror.co.uk/sport/other-sports/paralympian-sarah-storey-backs-mirrors-28535015

Cornish, P. (2021, August 25). *Where Does Dame Sarah Storey Live? Inside the Home of Paralympic Gold Medallist*. Express.co.uk. https://www.express.co.uk/life-style/property/1481676/where-does-Sarah-Storey-live-house-evg

Cosgrove, D. (2011, June 16). *Sarah Storey*. The Guardian. https://www.theguardian.com/sport/2011/jun/17/sarah-storey-100-hopefuls-for-2012

REFERENCES

CreativeMornings Sheffield. (2020, November 20). *Dame Sarah Storey for #CMtransit.* Www.youtube.com. Video, 0:58:25, https://www.youtube.com/watch?v=4k_Y-N83IUM

cyclingnewstv. (2015, May 11). *Dame Sarah Storey on Creating the Pearl Izumi Sports Tours Team.* Video. https://www.youtube.com/watch?v=4lpgbl85ki8

Dame Sarah Storey DBE. (n.d.). ParalympicsGB. The British Paralympic Association. Retrieved on August 2, 2023, from https://paralympics.org.uk/athletes/dame-sarah-storey-dbe

Dame Sarah Storey Keen to See 'tiered' Structure in Women's Cycling. (2015, July 6). Sky Sports. Sky News. https://www.skysports.com/more-sports/cycling/news/21683/9877721/dame-sarah-storey-keen-to-see-tiered-structure-in-womens-cycling

Dame Sarah Storey Talks Reaching Her Paralympic Dreams as She Poses with Her 17 Medals. (2021, September 12). Hello! Hello Magazine. https://www.hellomagazine.com/celebrities/20210912121441/sarah-storey-exclusive-interview-medals/

Deloitte UK. (2012, January 20). *Deloitte London 2012 Ambassador: Sarah Storey.* Video. https://www.youtube.com/watch?v=dv7lltdb1Fk

Duff, S. (2021, August 25). *From Swimmer to Winner: Who Is Dame Sarah Storey? Britain's Top Female Paralympics Athlete Scores First Gold Medal of Tokyo Games.* The U.S. Sun. August 25, 2021. https://www.the-sun.com/sport/3535703/who-is-dame-sarah-storey-paralympics-tokyo/

Family Affair: Running a Women's Cycling Team. (2017, June 10). TeamStoreySport; The Storey Racing Team. https://teamstoreysport.com/familyaffair/

Felix, A. (2019, May 22). *Allyson Felix: My Own Nike Pregnancy Story.* The New York Times. https://www.nytimes.com/video/opinion/100000006518461/allyson-felix-pregnancy-nike.html

Five Days to Go: Five Record-breaking Paralympians. (2023, June 27). Olympics.Com. https://olympics.com/en/news/five-days-to-go-five-record-breaking-paralympians

Fuller, A. (2021, December 13). *S3 Ep7: Dame Sarah Storey 'A problem shared is a problem halved.'* Monday Mile with Aimee Fuller (podcast). Retrieved on August 5, 2023, from https://open.spotify.com/episode/79UR5P4JspubIYgAOeU9ZA?si=Y2g83km3Q72Vr-NXsKgHgA

Gallacher, K. (2021, March 29). *Dame Sarah Storey.* Stripped Back Sport (podcast). Retrieved on August 5, 2023, from https://open.spotify.com/episode/505FbK1rsIIgqtFRJDBWLP?si=2cqJEj5uQ2-AUx95uhSZIA

Gender Equality in Sports Media. (n.d.). UNESCO: United Nations Educational, Scientific and Cultural Organization, Accessed August 23, 2023. https://webarchive.unesco.org/web/20230104165710/https://en.unesco.org/themes/gender-equality-sports-media#:~:text=Portrayal%20of%20Women%20in%20Sports%20Media&text=Media%20tend%20to%20represent%20women,dominating%2C%20and%20valued%20as%20athletes

Gordon, A., Joseph, A., & Williams, D. (2016, September 9). *God Save the Queen... Elsa! Dame Sarah Storey's Daughter Sang Let It Go from Frozen Instead of the National Anthem as Her Mother Became Britain's Most Successful Female Paralympian.* Daily Mail. https://www.dailymail.co.uk/news/article-3781695/God-Save-Queen-Elsa-Dame-Sarah-Storey-s-proud-husband-reveals-daughter-sang-Let-Frozen-instead-national-anthem-mother-Britain-s-successful-female-Paralympian.html

Greater Manchester Active Travel Commissioner. (n.d.). TeamStoreySport; The Storey Racing Team. Retrieved on August 28, 2023, from https://teamstoreysport.com/active-travel-commissioner/

REFERENCES

Guardian News. (2016, November 7). *Sarah Storey: How to Perform under Pressure*. Video. https://www.youtube.com/watch?v=A8Wl0SxIzao

Harle, T. (2023, August 3). *Storey Battles Through Biggest Challenge yet to Star at UCI World Championships*. SportsBeat. https://uk.sports.yahoo.com/news/storey-battles-through-biggest-challenge-yet-to-star-at-uci-world-championships-170546436.html?guccounter=1&guce_referrer=aHR0cHM6Ly93d3cuZ29vZ2xlLmNvbS8&guce_referrer_sig=AQAAAAaTafCBE3h4HKPhomzorx530Kfo56DdyYgeSVzo9owMVabNhJXAtOFZsPFOT2R6qrTdkxc7lR8bSCGzY6uAWbeGPNhlNAE4C7mbFIhVe-vBvkFm1B7BC1uuq-VHgkoq6eNSwuzuXDuiNXGIz7-pVzUVlugFkNzdY--tXzVvWbVo

Henson, M. (2012, September 5). *Paralympics 2012: Sarah Storey Wins Third London Gold*. BBC.Com. BBC Sport. https://www.bbc.com/sport/disability-sport/19487106

Herrero, C. P., Jejurikar, N., & Carter, C. W. (2021). The Psychology of the Female Athlete: How Mental Health and Wellness Mediate Sports Performance, Injury and Recovery. *Annals of Joint: An Open Access Journal for High-Quality Research in Bones and Joints, 6*. https://doi.org/10.21037/aoj-20-53

Hickmott, L. (2008, March 12). *Sarah Storey Pursuing More Paralympic Glory in Beijing*. Britishcycling.Org. British Cycling. https://web.archive.org/web/20091108180028/http://www.britishcycling.org.uk/web/site/BC/gbr/News2008/20080312_Sarah_Storey.asp

Hooper, A. (2022, July 23). *Dame Sarah Storey Hails 'First Step' to Cycling Equality as Tour De France Femmes Returns*. Mirror. https://www.mirror.co.uk/sport/other-sports/cycling/sarah-storey-tour-de-france-27546417

In This Extract from the Road Book 2021, Sarah Storey Describes Her Journey to Winning a Paralympic Gold Medal in the in the C4-5 Road Race. (2022, December 21). Rouleur. https://www.rouleur.cc/blogs/the-rouleur-journal/in-the-winners-words-dame-sarah-storey

Inspired Exchange. (2017, January 24). *Dame Sarah Storey Inspirational Speaker*. Video. https://www.youtube.com/watch?v=wqEQ6eAPuWc

Johnston, J. (2021, September 6). *'I Never Thought in Terms of Things I Couldn't Do': SARAH STOREY, Who Last Week Became Britain's Greatest Paralympian Ever, Reveals how She Masters Medal Winning AND Motherhood*. DailyMail. https://www.dailymail.co.uk/femail/article-9960285/How-master-medal-winning-motherhood-SARAH-STOREY.html

Kagel, E. (n.d.). *Congenital Hand Deformities*. EMK Orthopedics. Retrieved on August 7, 2023, from https://www.erickagelmd.com/hand-upper-extremity/congenital-hand-deformities/#:~:text=Congenital%20hand%20deformities%20may%20be,during%20the%20growth%20in%20womb

Kenton, N. (2019, September 11). *Sarah Storey on Paralympic Legacy, Motherhood and the Next Generation of Cyclists*. Independent. https://www.independent.co.uk/sport/olympics/paralympics/sarah-storey-cycling-paralympic-games-tokyo-japan-olympics-world-championship-a9099246.html

Kidd, S. (2013, October 11). *A Glossary of Cycling Events: Road, Off-Road, and Track Racing*. Breaking Muscle. https://breakingmuscle.com/a-glossary-of-cycling-events-road-off-road-and-track-racing/

Laker, L, & Boulting, N. (2022, March 17) *Dame Sarah Storey: Streets Ahead* (podcast). Retrieved on August 28, 2023, from https://open.spotify.com/episode/4BVdf03VNBwourTlJ8n48y?si=0SkEj-WgQqepl8E07YloEA

Lapp, L., & Davidson, L. (2020, April 21). *Resilience: The Ways To Enhance This Critical Skill In Sports*. Broadway Psychology. http://broadviewpsychology.com/2020/04/21/resilience-the-

REFERENCES

ways-to-enhance-this-critical-skill-in-sports/#:~:text=Resilient%20athletes%20develop%
20confidence%20in%20their%20ability%20to%20recover%20and%20overcome%
20hardships.&text=Being%20willing%20and%20open%20to,can%20go%20a%20long%20way

Le Col. (2022, February 18). *Mental Preparation With Dame Sarah Storey.* Video. https://www.
youtube.com/watch?v=az8bvmDl0Ew

Lee, A. (2013, October 1). *Paralympic Gold Medalist Sarah Storey: Cycling Helped Me Recover after
Giving Birth.* Express.co.uk. https://www.express.co.uk/life-style/health/433520/
Paralympic-gold-medalist-Sarah-Storey-Cycling-helped-me-recover-after-giving-birth#

Legend: Sarah Storey. (2021, July 27). www.youtube.com; GNC Plus. Video, 0:01:13, https://
youtu.be/VzeXj1BVJNw

Lloyd, M. (2021, July 27). *Legend: Dame Sarah Storey.* Global Cycling Network. 55 min. https://
plus.globalcyclingnetwork.com/watch/2867357

MacInnes, P. (2021, August 20). *Sarah Storey Closes on Outright British Paralympic Record after Time
Trial Gold.* The Guardian. https://www.theguardian.com/sport/2021/aug/31/sarah-storey-
closes-on-outright-british-paralympic-record-after-time-trial-gold

Manchester Metropolitan University. (2018, August 13). *Dame Sarah Storey on Training in
Manchester Metropolitan's Environment Chamber.* Video. https://www.youtube.com/watch?v=
Hzrmj-WD4wo

McRae, D. (2015, January 19). *Sarah Storey: Because of the Pain You Might Never Want to Do It
Again.* The Guardian. https://www.theguardian.com/sport/2015/jan/19/sarah-storey-
british-paralympian-womens-cycling-hour-record

Mercer, D. (2021, September 2). *Dame Sarah Storey: How Cyclist Overcame Bullying and Eating
Disorder to Become Britain's Greatest Paralympian.* Sky News. https://news.sky.com/story/
dame-sarah-storey-how-cyclist-overcame-bullying-and-eating-disorder-to-become-britains-
greatest-female-paralympian-12389429

Merriam-Webster. (n.d.). *Definition of RESILIENCE.* Accessed September 12, 2023. https://www.
merriam-webster.com/dictionary/resilience

Non-executive Board Member: DfT Dame Sarah Storey. (n.d.). Gov.uk. UK Governent. Retrieved on
August 28, 2023, from https://www.gov.uk/government/people/sarah-storey#:~:text=In%
202019%20she%20was%20appointed,region%27s%20second%20Active%20Travel%
20Commissioner

Oldham Council. (2023, July 4). *First School Street Opens in Oldham with Dame Sarah Storey.* Video,
0:02:24. https://www.youtube.com/watch?v=IPxAVg0u7w4

Packham, A. (2017, November 1). *Fit Fix: Dame Sarah Storey Reflects On What It Takes To Become
The Most Successful British Female Paralympian.* HuffPost. The Huffington Post. https://www.
huffingtonpost.co.uk/entry/sarah-storey-motivation-career_uk_59f098cce4b0e064db7e1913.

Parker, I. (2023, August 14). *Dame Sarah Storey Wins 42nd World Title with Time Trial Success in
Dumfries.* Independent. https://www.independent.co.uk/sport/cycling/sarah-storey-
dumfries-cycling-b2391099.html

Pearson, E., & Misener, L. (2021, September 1). *Paralympians Still Don't Get the Kind of Media
Attention They Deserve as Elite Athletes.* The Conversation. https://theconversation.com/
paralympians-still-dont-get-the-kind-of-media-attention-they-deserve-as-elite-athletes-166879

Performance People. (2023, April 10). *Dame Sarah Storey + Barney Storey: In Tandem | Performance
People.* In *www.youtube.com.* https://www.youtube.com/watch?v=I90eaNZ7fx8

Roberts, O. (2022, July 23). *Tour De France Femmes: Sarah Storey Reveals She'D Love to Compete in*

Race. GiveMeSport. https://www.givemesport.com/88038142-tour-de-france-femmes-sarah-storey-reveals-shed-love-to-compete-in-race/

RoryOConnorTV. (2016, December 15). *Dame Sarah Storey Interview | Pride of Sport Awards 2016*. Video. https://www.youtube.com/watch?v=Z6egeFV1FxY

Rosa, C. (2021, February 3). *Dame Sarah Storey DBE*. Driving Force (podcast). Retrieved on August 5, 2023, from https://open.spotify.com/episode/2osMDfKZTK4o5Ax705iPIx?si=-CytRQ_jThCI18kxht9sSw

Rossmeier, V. (2009, September 14). *Did Motherhood Help Clijsters Win?* Salon. https://www.salon.com/2009/09/14/pregnancy_2/

Sarah Storey. (n.d.). TeamStoreySport. Retrieved on August 11, 2023, from https://teamstoreysport.com/sarah-storey/

Sarah's Frequently Asked Questions. (n.d.) TeamStoreySport. Retrieved on August 11, 2023, from https://teamstoreysport.com/sarahs-frequently-asked-questions/

Sarkar, M. & and Fletcher, D. (2014, April 9). Psychological resilience in sport performers: a review of stressors and protective factors. *Journal of Sports Sciences*. 32(15), 1419–1434. https://10.1080/02640414.2014.901551

Schools' Climate Education South Yorkshire. (2021, July 5). *Welcome Address - Dame Sarah Storey | SCESY 2021*. Video. https://www.youtube.com/watch?v=S9NZi6_h-Yw

ŠKoda UK. (2022, July 6). *Dame Sarah Storey on the Tour De France Femme 2022 | ŠKODA DSI Cycling Academy*. Www.youtube.com. Video, 0:01:02. https://youtu.be/-X24wIN4rGo

Sky Sports News. (2021, September 3). *Dame Sarah Storey on Becoming the Most Successful British Paralympian*. Video. https://youtu.be/bRcdc6DCquc?si=EwjQFeuYf0-1SvIN

Snape, J. (2021, September 1). *Mastermind: Dame Sarah Storey*. Inside the Mind of Champions (podcast). Retrieved on August 8, 2023, from https://open.spotify.com/episode/2e1ojyTX2MfT8N6UkwupxI?si=UEUcVUNRRoexkQn-9AQ0Rg

Spender, J., & Cole, E. (2022, February 17). *49: Dame Sarah Storey Is as Inspiring as You'd Imagine*. Cyclist Magazine Podcast (podcast). Retrieved on August 5, 2023, from https://open.spotify.com/episode/1l6pHejHWJsOATX385MhRZ?si=4fMQZ_UWR52avZ9mIchtow&context=spotify%3Ashow%3A6yTmEK9cJ0VHjSs5G9hrpZ

Sporting Edge. (2014, June 25). *Dame Sarah Storey - What Is Resilience?* Video. https://www.youtube.com/watch?v=_QwE2HVVXCk

Sporting Heritage. (2022, October 22). *Dame Sarah Storey, DBE - Keynote Presentation 2020*. Video. https://www.youtube.com/watch?v=8m-2UYiLxe4

Sports Journalists' Association. (2020, December 10). *The SJA Bill McGowran Trophy: Dame Sarah Storey*. Video. https://www.youtube.com/watch?v=LekDXI3YEWM

Steinberg, J. (2016, September 17). *Sarah Storey Wins 14th Paralympic Gold in Women's Road Race in Rio*. The Guardian. https://www.theguardian.com/sport/2016/sep/17/sarah-storey-gold-cycling-womens-road-race-rio-2016-paralympics

Stevenson, J. (2013, April 25). *Interview: Dame Sarah Storey, GB's Most Decorated Female Paralympian*. TotalWomensCycling. https://totalwomenscycling.com/lifestyle/interviews/interview-dame-sarah-storey-gbs-most-decorated-female-paralympian

Storey Channel. (2023a, February 13). *Netball Superleague Season Opener*. Video. https://youtu.be/yPRtZptiftg?si=6fwKflBscnMP5y9v

Storey Channel. (2023b, February 21). *Louisa Challenges Mum to a Race!* Video. https://www.youtube.com/watch?v=rBZ_QBLKQ7E

REFERENCES

Storey Channel. (2023c, February 27). *How Not to Bonk!* Www.youtube.com. Video. https://youtu.be/0LB9PyBEX8c?si=yadkTgxdcd_iZ44H

Storey, S. (2022). Refreshing Greater Manchester's Active Travel Mission. In *Transport for Greater Manchester*. Retrieved on August 30, 2023, from https://assets.ctfassets.net/xfhv954w443t/2KKdqfwHfYhAZZI0Lydgb/c0fc1bc034562b77869c7e94787c871a/Greater_Manchester-s_Active_Travel_Mission.pdf

Storey, S. (2023a, March). *Earlier This Week I Joined the Wheels For All Session at Debdale Park...* [Post]. LinkedIn. https://www.linkedin.com/posts/dame-sarah-storey-03a03025_earlier-this-week-i-joined-the-wheels-for-activity-7045130482874748928-krHT?utm_source=share&utm_medium=member_desktop

Storey, S. (2023b, March 10). *Pretty Cool First Day Back at Work after Time off for Holidays & to Recharge!...* [Post] LinkedIn. https://www.linkedin.com/posts/dame-sarah-storey-03a03025_pretty-cool-first-day-back-at-work-after-activity-7104215523491536896-FvFI?utm_source=share&utm_medium=member_ios

Storey, S. (2023c, March 10). *School Streets Are about Making It Safer for Children on Their Journeys to and from School, but the Extra Activity They Enable Also Builds Confidence and Sets Everyone up for a Positive Day/Evening...* [Post] LinkedIn. https://www.linkedin.com/posts/dame-sarah-storey-03a03025_school-activetravel-activity-7040066510832185344-COVd?utm_source=share&utm_medium=member_desktop

Storey, S. (2023d, June). *What a Way to Finish off My #BikeWeek Activity!* [Post] LinkedIn. https://www.linkedin.com/posts/dame-sarah-storey-03a03025_bikeweek-bikefridedays-bikebus-activity-7073048865368592384-xlGk?utm_source=share&utm_medium=member_ios

Storey, S. (2023e, July). *Visiting Councils that Are Pulling Together a Bigger Plan and Knitting Together the Many Facets of an Integrated Active Travel and Public Transport System.* [Post] LinkedIn. https://www.linkedin.com/posts/dame-sarah-storey-03a03025_activetravel-schoolstreets-bikelibrary-activity-7082459120494080002-5z0O?utm_source=share&utm_medium=member_ios

Storey Takes 17th World Championship Title to Lead Great Britain Medal Rush on Day Eight in Scotland. (2023, August 10). British Cycling. https://www.britishcycling.org.uk/gbcyclingteam/article/20230810-gb-cyclingteam-news-Storey-takes-17th-world-championship-title-to-lead-medal-rush-on-day-eight-in-Scotland-0

SuperPopVIP. (2013, December 4). *INTERVIEW: Sarah Storey on It Being an Honour, Meeting Al...* Video. https://www.youtube.com/watch?v=XSvR0fdVR9k

Thurston, E. (2021, December 1). *Dame Sarah Storey Speaks About Her Experience of Bullying and Disordered Eating.* Sky Sports. Sky Sports. https://www.skysports.com/more-sports/other-sports/news/29177/12182221/dame-sarah-storey-speaks-about-her-experience-of-bullying-and-disordered-eating

Tokyo Paralympics: Sarah Storey Wins 15th Paralympic Gold as GB Claim Six Medals. (2021, August 25). BBC.Com. BBC Sport. https://www.bbc.com/sport/disability-sport/58326267

Transport for Greater Manchester. (2023, June 6). *Dame Sarah Storey Sets Out Vision Zero Commitment to Prevent Deaths and Serious Injuries.* Greater Manchester Moving. https://www.gmmoving.co.uk/news/dame-sarah-storey-sets-out-vision-zero-commitment-to-prevent-deaths-and-serious-injuries

UCI. (2015a, February 28). *#UCIHourRecord - Dame Sarah Storey - "The Hardest Hour of My Life."* Video, 0:02:13. https://www.youtube.com/watch?v=bi5awJj7KCE

REFERENCES

UCI. (2015b, February 28). *Full Replay - #UCIHourRecord Dame Sarah Storey - London 2015*. Www.youtube.com. Video, 1:32:08. https://www.youtube.com/watch?v=K8tgGIb24Hk

University of Brighton. (2016, September 9). *Sarah Storey*. Video. https://youtu.be/8x_36Z03KgQ?si=BRG76gbt7LOCD4Bh

Voxwomen. (2015, March 1). *News - Dame Sarah Storey Hour Record Attempt*. Video. https://www.youtube.com/watch?v=mKuDQ6wYyY8

Voxwomen. (2017, May 1). *Top Tips with Dame Sarah Storey*. Video. https://www.youtube.com/watch?v=8HgMfnCzVKM

Warwick, M. (2021, February 22). *Dame Sarah Storey Searching for Amateur Female Talent to Join Pro Peloton*. BBC Sport. BBC. https://www.bbc.co.uk/sport/cycling/56125486

Welch, B. (2022, July 18). *A Brief History of the 'Women's Tour De France.'* Velo. https://velo.outsideonline.com/news/a-brief-history-of-the-womens-tour-de-france/#

Welcome to Wheels for All. (n.d.). Wheels for All. Accessed September 12, 2023. https://wheelsforall.org.uk/

Wray, A. (2021, July 10). *Being a Professional Athlete or Motherhood: The Struggles and Strides*. Sports as Told by a Girl. https://www.sportsastoldbyagirl.com/being-a-professional-athlete-or-motherhood-the-struggles-and-strides/